THE HABITS TO BE SUCCESSFUL IN LIFE

Learn How to Achieve Greatest Heights in your Life and Career from the Most Successful People of the World

By

HENRY JAMESON

2

INTRODUCTION

When working on his doctorate in the 1970s, Stephen R. Covey studied 200 years of productive literature. He found that since the 1920s, popular writings have concentrated on approaches to specific problems. For certain cases, such tactical guidance might have been helpful, but only for immediate concerns and not for long-term structural problems. In the last half of the 20th century, good literature usually attributes the performance to personalities, skills, strategies, a positive mindset, etc. This philosophy may be referred to as the ethic of personality.

Nevertheless, over the 150 years or so preceding that time, the literature on performance was more characteristically focused. It underscored the deeper principles and foundations of success. This philosophy is known as the Ethical Character, in which achievement is more related to underlying characteristics such as honesty, bravery, fairness, endurance, etc.

The elements of Character Ethics are primary features, while those of Personality Ethics are secondary. Although secondary traits that enable one to play the game in order to succeed in some particular circumstances, both are important for long-term success. One character is the most obvious factor in long-term relationships. Why are you shouting so loudly in my ears that I can't hear what you're doing?

Covey gives the following definition to explain the distinction between primary and secondary traits. Suppose you 're in Chicago and you're using a map to find a specific destination in the city. You may have outstanding secondary skills in map reading and navigation, but if you use the Detroit map, you can never find your destination. In this case, getting the right map is a crucial element before your secondary skills can be used effectively.

The problem with relying on personality ethics is that, unless the basic underlying paradigms are right, simply modifying external behavior is not successful. We see a world based on our experience, which can have a drastic effect on the way we see things. For example, there have been several studies in which two groups of people have seen two different drawings. For example, a drawing of a young, beautiful woman is shown in one group, and a drawing of an aged, delicate woman is shown in the other. After the initial exposure to the drawings, an image of a more abstract drawing is displayed to both classes. Interestingly, this drawing incorporates the characteristics of both the young woman and the older woman. Nearly always, someone in the audience seen for the first time by a young woman sees a young woman in an abstract drawing, and those seen by an older woman see an older woman. Each party was persuaded that the drawing was critically evaluated. The argument is that we do not see things as they are, but because we are programmed to see them. When we have realized the importance of our past experiences, we will undergo a paradigm change in the way we see things. To order to make significant changes in our lives, we need to focus on the fundamental paradigms through which we can see the universe.

Character Ethics suggests that there are certain basic values that reside among all human beings. Examples of these values include justice, honesty, integrity, human dignity, efficiency, potential, and development. Principles are for particular cases as opposed to procedures in those circumstances, whereas principles are for universal application.

Our character is a set of our habits, and our habits have an important role to play in our lives. The habits are knowledge, ability, and desire. Awareness helps us to know what to do, talent gives us the opportunity to learn how to do it, and ambition is the inspiration to do it.

Most of today's popular literature seems to respect individuality, to empower people to become free, and to do their own thing. The truth is that we are interdependent, and an autonomous model is not suitable for use in an interdependent setting that involves leadership and team members.

In order to make it possible to be interdependent, one must first be self-reliant, because dependent people have not yet established the character of interdependence. The first three habits, therefore, concentrate on self-mastery: achieving the private victories required to transition from dependency to independence. The first three customs are as follows:

- ✓ Habit 1: Be Proactive

- ✓ Habit 2: Begin with the End in Mind

- ✓ Habit 3: Put First Things First

Habits 4, 5, and 6 then address interdependence:

- ✓ Habit 4: Think Win/Win

- ✓ Habit 5: Seek First to Understand, Then to Be Understood

- ✓ Habit 6: Synergize

At the end of the day, the seventh habit is one of regeneration and continuous improvement, that is, of creating one's own personal production capacity. In order to be successful, one must find the right balance between actually producing and improving one's production ability. Covey illustrates this point with a fairy tale of goose and golden egg.

In the fable, the poor farmer's goose began to lay a solid gold egg every day, and the farmer soon became wealthy. He also became greedy and felt that the goose must have a lot of golden eggs inside her. So get all the eggs right away, he killed the goose. As he sliced it open, he found that it wasn't full of golden eggs. The lesson is that if one tries to increase immediate production without regard to production efficiency, the efficiency will be lost. Effectiveness is a function of both demand and production efficiency.

The need for a balance between demand and production efficiency relates to physical, financial, and human properties. For example, a person in control of a particular machine can increase the immediate performance of the machine by postponing routine maintenance. This person will be rewarded with promotion as a result of improved performance. Nevertheless, the improved immediate performance will come at the cost of potential production, as further maintenance would have to be carried out on the machine later. The person who inherits the mess can also be blamed for the unavoidable downtime and high maintenance costs.

Consumer satisfaction is also an advantage to which the balance of demand and production efficiency relates. A restaurant may have a reputation for serving great food, but the owner may want to reduce the cost and lower the quality of the food. Immediately profits will increase, but soon the prestige of the restaurant will disappear, the confidence of the customer will be lost, and profits will decline.

This does not mean that it is only generating capacity that is important. If one builds ability, but never uses it, there will be no manufacture. There is a compromise between building up production capacity and actually generating power. Finding the right tradeoff is crucial to one's performance.

WHAT PARADIGMS ARE

Have you ever paused to remember all the little bits that make up the society you live in? There are, of course, many traditions and institutions, like public schools, but what about the beliefs you express with those around you, like friends and family? These thoughts, principles, and values that you and others share about religion, ethnicity, and other aspects of culture are obviously a major part of your individual and collective identities, But how much do you think about where they come from or how they could adjust?

A set of beliefs and principles is what is known as a paradigm, a collection of hypotheses, assumptions, and ideas that relate to your worldview or establish a context through which you function every day. For example, you may have used the word, 'American way of life,' which is a metaphor because it applies to a set of values and ideas about what it means to be American. To people who consider this concept very important, it may serve as a basis for how they perceive or communicate with the world around them. This underlines one of the most important aspects of the model, which is that it is made up of values and ideas that form a basis for approaching and communicating with certain issues or individuals.

The terms model and theory are often used interchangeably in social science, but social scientists do not necessarily accept that they are similar or distinct. In this chapter, I will make a clear distinction between the two concepts, since thinking of each term as analytically distinct offers a useful context for understanding the ties between research methods and social science thought.

PARADIGMS IN SOCIAL SCIENCE

For our purposes, we describe paradigm as a way of looking at the world (or an "analytical lens" like a pair of glasses) and a structure for interpreting human experience. It can be difficult to fully understand the concept of paradigmatic assumptions since we are profoundly rooted in our own, intimate, daily way of thinking. Let's look at people's views on abortion, for example. For some, contraception is a medical procedure that should be performed at the discretion of each individual woman. For others, abortion is murder, and members of society should have a collective right to decide when, if at all, abortion should take place. Chances are, if you have an opinion on this topic, you 're pretty confident about the veracity of your viewpoint. Again, the person who sits next to you in class can have a completely different viewpoint and yet be equally sure in the reality of their perspective. Who's right?

You are each working under a collection of assumptions about the way the world does — or should at least do — work. Perhaps your conclusions come from your political viewpoint, which tends to influence your opinion on a number of social topics, or whether your perceptions are based on what you have heard from your parents or in the church. There is, in any case, a paradigm that shapes your position on the matter. These paradigms are a collection of assumptions. Your classmate may believe that life begins at birth and that the life of the fetus should be at the core of the moral study. Conversely, you may believe that life starts when the fetus is viable outside the womb and that the option of a mother is more important than the life of a fetus. There is no way to test scientifically when life begins, the interests of which are more important, or the value of choice. These are simply philosophic conclusions or convictions. Thus, the pro-life paradigm can rely partly on the belief in divine morality and fetal rights. A pro-choice philosophy may be based on a mother's self-determination and the assumption that the positive effects of abortion outweigh the negative ones. These beliefs and assumptions influence how we think about any aspect of the matter.

Paradigms are a way to describe what we know, what we know, and how we know it. There are many prevalent paradigms in social science, each with its own particular ontological and epistemological perspective. Note that ontology is a study of what is real, and epistemology is a study of how we come to learn what is real. Let's look at four of the most popular social science paradigms that might help you when you start thinking about research.

The first theory that we will discuss, called positivism, is the concept that is likely to come to mind for many of you when you think about science. Positivism is motivated by the concepts of objectivity, intelligence, and deductive inference. Deductive logic is explored in more detail in the following section of this essay. The positivist paradigm is based on the assumption that society can and should be observed empirically and scientifically. Positivism often calls for value-free science, one in which researchers aim to abandon their beliefs and ideals in pursuit of empirical, empiric, and informed reality.

Social constructionism is another prevalent concept of social work. Peter Berger and Thomas Luckman (1966) are credited to many for developing this perspective in sociology. Although positivists are looking for "the facts," the social-constructive approach claims that "the facts" differ. Truth is different from who you ask, and people change their definitions of truth all the time based on their interactions with other people. This is because, according to this theory, we construct facts ourselves (as opposed to merely existing and trying to uncover it) through our experiences and our perceptions of those interactions. The secret to the social constructionist viewpoint is the belief that social meaning and interaction are the basis of our realities.

Scholars working within this context have a particular interest in how people come to a collective consensus, or disagree, on what is real and valid. Consideration of how the meanings of various hand gestures vary in different regions of the world is appropriately illustrated by the social and cultural creation of meanings. Think about what it means to you when you see a person raising their middle finger. We probably all know that the person is not very happy (nor is the person to whom the finger is being directed). For some cultures, it is another gesture, like a thumbs-up gesture, that raises the eyebrows. Although a thumb-up gesture can have a special significance in North American culture, the significance is not spread across cultures. So, what's the "real" of the middle finger or the thumbs up? This depends on what the person giving this meant, how it was perceived by the person receiving it, and the social context in which the action took place.

This would be misleading to think of the social constructionist viewpoint as simply individualistic. Although individuals that build their own narratives, groups — from small ones like married couples to large ones like nations — often agree on notions of what is true and what "is." In other words, the concepts that we build have power over the individual people who establish them. As a result, the ways in which individuals and societies work to build and alter these definitions are of as much interest to social constructionists as the manner in which they were first created.

The third model is the main one. At its heart, the essential framework focuses on wealth, injustice, and social change. Although some very diverse viewpoints are included here, the critical model typically incorporates ideas developed by early social theorists, such as Max Horkheimer, and later works developed by feminist scholars. Unlike the positivist model, the critical paradigm claims that social science can never be fully empirical or value-free. Therefore, this concept functions from the viewpoint that scientific work should be performed with the explicit goal of social change in mind. Critical paradigm researchers may begin with the awareness that structures are biased toward, for example, women or ethnic minorities. In addition, their research projects are planned not only to collect data but also to alter the research participants and the processes under review. The essential model not only explores power imbalances but aims to alter these power imbalances.

Postmodernism is, ultimately, a philosophy that contradicts almost every way of knowing that many social scientists take for granted. While the positivists argue that there is an objective, known truth, the postmodernists will suggest that there is no fact. While social-constructionists might claim that the truth is in the viewer's eye (or in the viewer's eye), postmodernists might claim that we can never truly know the truth since, through observing and recording the truths of others, the researcher sets his own reality to the investigation. Finally, while the critical paradigm would assert that power, inequality, and change shape reality and truth, the post-modernist can also question the force, inequality, change, reality, and truth of whose power. As you might expect, the post-modern model is quite a challenge for researchers. Why do you research something that may or may not be real, or is that only possible in your present and special experience? This interesting topic is worth exploring when you begin to think about conducting your own work. Part of the value of the post-modern model is its focus on the limitations of human knowledge.

Let's work by way of an example. When we look at an issue such as substance abuse, what would the social scientific inquiry look like in every paradigm? Positivist studies can focus on precisely measuring substance abuse and identifying key causes of substance abuse during adolescence. Forgetting the objectivity of precisely measuring substance abuse, a social construction study might focus on how people who abuse substances understand their lives and their relationships with various drug abuse drugs. In doing so, it seeks out the subjective truth of each participant in the study. A critical paradigm study will explore how people who have substance abuse problems are a marginalized group in society and try to free them from external sources of oppression, such as draconian drug laws and internal sources of oppression, such as internalized fear and shame. Post-modern studies can include a person's self-reported path to substance abuse and changes in self-perception that have followed their transition from leisure to problematic drug use. Such examples will show how one topic can be explored through each model.

Social Science Theories

Like paradigms, theories provide a way to look at the world and understand human interaction. Paradigms are grounded in great assumptions about the world — what is real, how do we create knowledge — whereas theories describe more specific phenomena. A common concept of the theory of social work is "a structured collection of interlinked statements to describe certain aspects of social life. At its core, theories can be used to provide explanations for any number or variety of phenomena. These help us answer the "why" questions that we always have about the trends we experience in social life. The theories also help us to answer our "how" questions. While paradigms that point us in a particular direction when it comes to our "Why" questions, theories more precisely map out the reason or the "How" behind the "Why" question.

Introductory textbooks for social work introduce students to core social work theories — theory of conflict, symbolic interaction, the theory of social exchange, and systems theory. As social workers research longer, more concrete ideas are implemented in their area of interest, as well as viewpoints and models (e.g., strengths perspective) that offer more practice-oriented approaches to understanding social work.

As you would probably remember from the Social Work Theory class, systems theorists interpret all aspects of society as interconnected and concentrate on the interactions, boundaries, and energy flows between these processes and subsystems. Conflict theorists are interested in questions of control and who wins and who loses on the basis of the way society is structured. Symbolic interactionists concentrate on how meaning is created and mediated through substantive (i.e., symbolic) interactions. Social exchange theories, ultimately, investigate how human beings base their actions on a fair measurement of rewards and costs.

Much like researchers could look at the same subject from various levels of study or paradigms, they could also look at the same subject from different theoretical perspectives. In this situation, even their study questions may be the same, but the way they make sense of the phenomenon they are researching would primarily be influenced by theory.

There are many other theories within each area of social work specialization that aim to explain more specific types of interactions. For example, in the context of sexual assault, various theories offer different reasons as to why assault is happening. One theory, first formulated by criminologists, is called the theory of daily activitiesSexual harassment is argued for if no organized organizations are involved and if possible vulnerable targets and motivated perpetrators exist. Many theories of sexual assault, called relational theories, say that a person's relationships, such as partnerships or friendships, are crucial to understanding why and how sexual harassment occurs in the workplace and how people react to it when it happens. Relational theories concentrate on the influence of various social relationships (e.g., married people who have supportive partners at home may be more likely than those who lack support at home to report sexual assault when it happens). Finally, feminist explanations of sexual assault have a different perspective. Such hypotheses indicate that the structure of our existing gender system, where the most dominant are the men, better explains when and how sexual assault happens in the workplace. As you would expect, the researchers' questions of harassment are influenced by the researchers' theory of sexual harassment. It will also form the reasons the researcher provides as to why harassment is occurring.

It might be overwhelming for an undergraduate student to begin learning a new topic and know that there are so many hypotheses beyond what you have studied in your theory classes. Worse, there is no central database of different theories on your subject. However, when you study the literature in your subject field, you can learn more about the ideas that scientists have developed to explain how your subject functions in the real world. In addition to peer-reviewed journal articles, a book on your subject is another valuable source of theory. Books also include works of theoretical and philosophical significance outside the scope of an academic journal.

PARADIGM AND THEORY IN SOCIAL WORK

The hypotheses, paradigms, levels of study, and the order in which one continues in the research process all play a significant role in influencing what we ask about the social environment, how we ask it, and, in some cases, what we are likely to discover. A micro-level analysis of gangs would look very different from a macro-level analysis of gangs. In some cases, you may be able to apply multiple levels of analysis to your investigation, but doing so is not always practical or feasible. It is, therefore, crucial to understand the different levels of analysis and to be aware of the level at which you are employing. Research would also form one's theoretical perspective. In fact, it is possible that the hypothesis discussed would influence not only the way a question is posed about the subject but also the topic that will be explored in the first place. Furthermore, if you find yourself particularly committed to one theory over another, it may limit the kind of questions you ask. As a consequence, other potential theories could be lacking.

The shortcomings of paradigms and hypotheses do not mean that social science is inherently biased. At the same time, we can never claim to be completely free of value. Social constructionists and postmodernists might point out that bias is always part of at least some degree of research. Our role as researchers is to identify and resolve our prejudices, if imperfect, as part of the research process. We all use our own approaches, be they theories, levels of analysis, or time processes, to frame and carry out our work. Knowing such structures and methods is important not just for the effective launch and completion of any research-based inquiry, but also for the informed reading and interpretation of the work of others.

BEST PRINCIPLES FOR SUCCESS YOU NEED TO HAVE IN YOUR LIFE

Success is something we all want to achieve. It's a way of life that we're dreaming about. Why don't you want to shoot for the stars, hit your targets, and enjoy the sweet life you've worked so hard to achieve? That's why Elite Daily talked to the experts to give you the 411 on the best principles of success that you should keep in hand.

The performance will come down to the ideals that you live by to make your dreams a reality. Personally, I assume that progress has been accomplished with three others: policy, funding, and administration. The strategy is the 'how.' Although it's relevant, you don't need all the specifics [from the start]. Aid is the 'who.' If you want to make a successful success, you'll need help getting there. The state (of being) is the 'why,' knowing why you want this success first. You have a clear vision in your mind as to why you can be guided towards your goals.

It is important to remember that the concept of "performance" can differ for each person. That being said, here are 13 values that will help you achieve the goals you 're working for.

BE COMMITTED.

Only the most prepared-for-travel may have unforeseen twists and turns. Being completely dedicated is a crucial component to achieving your final destination, irrespective of hitting any bumps on the way.

Celebrate the successes, but realize that they're not the destination. You [can] pick up after your defeats, knowing that they are not the ends of your dreams. Take the "slow and steady" path. Your personal path to success is not a competition.

DO EXACTLY WHAT MAKES YOU LOVE YOURSELF.

Do what makes you enjoy yourself. "It's just so important to fill your life with things that make you happy about who you are. When you're not enthusiastic about what you're doing, it's easy to get sick of your situation easily. If you do what makes you enjoy yourself, you can feel more balanced and coordinated.

SET AN ATTAINABLE ROUTINE.

People set goals, have ambitions, and want different things in life, but they may not be able to accomplish them if they don't really start working for them. Never put things off until tomorrow. Begin by setting a simple, attainable routine today. Take some move, collect input. The right way, repeat.

There are several advantages to setting up a daily routine. Scheduling time for exercise and balanced eating will fill the body with energy and nutrients for the day. Having a good sleep can make you feel rejuvenated and can affect your body and mind. The article also notes that the organization will lead to less stress and anxiety in general. Positive practice can lead to positive outcomes.

MOVE-IN THE RIGHT DIRECTION.

You might find yourself asking, how can I tell you if I'm going in the 'right' direction to achieve my goals? Going in the "right" direction means that you feel fully in line with your feelings, emotions, and actions. It means what you think, how you feel, and what you will function in harmony. The way you 're going is supposed to feel perfect. There will be many changes in life, and you may need to reassess your path.

USE THE POWER OF DREAMS AND YOUR IMAGINATION.

You're still a kid with crazy dreams and a strong imagination, "so have fun. What you're dreaming of is what you should make happen in your life.

Life has rules and structure; there's no creativity. By combining achievement expectations with the widest possible use of our fantasy, we can tap into an inspiring source. "But don't get too embedded in dreaming and imagining without that.

THINK BIGGER THAN YOU ARE.

Think bigger, always. It's important to bear in mind that unexpected curveballs will come your way, and while a lot of things can be done if you put your mind to them, things may not go according to plan. The key is to set up a happy medium when it comes to thinking. Dream and dream high, but have a good dose of truth to compensate for that.

FOCUS ON GROWTH.

Success is a problem-solving, solution-driven scenario, and this is where development comes from. Circumstances can change as you move through life. Things don't always go as you planned, but you learn and develop along the way. Face it: Even when you're going through a tough time, you can figure it out, take a valuable lesson, and grow that much stronger in the process.

BE DETERMINED.

Where there's a will, there's a way — even if you've got to build one. [Have] patience in action, commitment for the goal, and endurance to resolve. And if there are challenges or the path doesn't go at the speed you 'd like it to go, you 're always persevering in the direction of the goals: "It's not about thinking hard, feeling committed, [and] putting your mind on stuff. It's about participating in the millions of acts that are typically expected to succeed.

HAVE A CLEAR VISION IN MIND.

Success is about vision. Vision is going to help you to see where you need to go. Your dream should be a blueprint for what you're actually going to do to [achieve] success. He points out that clarification is important.

SET GOALS ALONG THE WAY.

The final aim is to build a big picture and see the finished canvas. Your objectives are the color you use to get there. To make sure you stay on the right path, create "checkpoints." You can change that way if you ever end up going off track. Such goals can be broken down into three categories: easy-to-achieve short-term goals, mid-term goals that allow you to be committed, and long-term goals that depend on both your short-term and mid-term goals. "Short-term goals are the motivating fuel that helps us to remain in the game to reach long-term goals.

USE AFFIRMATIONS TO KEEP MOTIVATED.

Affirmations are what motivate you on your journey. You describe your own truth with affirmations. There's a lot of strength to constantly say supportive things like, "I have this," "I can do this," and "I want this." You 're building a constructive conversation for yourself, and this positive attitude will ultimately become a reality. Edwards continues, "It doesn't matter what, you can always say, '[I] can.'

SURROUND YOURSELF WITH PEOPLE WHO GENUINELY SUPPORT YOU.

Negative factors and negative people will stand in the way of you. On your road to success, do your hardest to get rid of toxic energy. You 're just as strong as the people who love you. "Surround yourself with people who believe in you and are excited about your dreams.

You can tell whether a friend or loved one is sincerely supportive whether they care for you, and not just your dream of success. "People who are enamored by your dream for themselves only, for their future only, and not for the happiness that gives, at best, you are short-term supporters.

APPRECIATE EVERYTHING YOU ALREADY HAVE IN YOUR LIFE.

The ultimate idea of success is to value what you already have. Realize that you've always had plenty, and be grateful for what your future looks like. Feeling appreciative and thankful for what you've got keeps you focused, encourages you to appreciate the moment, and helps keep you optimistic. The more appreciative you are of what you have, the more enthusiastic you are going to grow vs. fear of not getting enough.

THE HABITS OF MOST SUCCESSFUL PEOPLE

The list has little to do with patterns, focused on established ideals of well-being, transparency, honesty, dignity, and human development. Here are the seven patterns of highly successful people, as our experts have observed.

1. THEY PRIORITIZE PHYSICAL AND MENTAL WELLNESS

The most popular habit is to concentrate on the important, not the urgent, stuff. There are few more critical things than one's wellbeing – but safety is easily overlooked, as the effects are often felt in the long run.

The physical benefits of exercise are well known. Yet the advantages of exercise are much more than mere physical exercise. Team sports include being part of something bigger than yourself – celebrating a goal made by a friend, or moving on to someone else – qualities that are desperately lacking in the business world. Community fitness courses harness motivation from those around you, and a trainer gives a vital mental break as opposed to trying to motivate yourself. Also, solo exercise, such as biking, is a refreshing break from relentless email bombing. Even having a workout planned later in the day makes you more successful because you know you have something to look forward to.

Wellness is much more than mere exercise. While practically everyone knows what healthy eating means, few have put it into action, and the developing world is becoming increasingly obese. The idea that you need to be constantly on email means that you can't ever relax, even on holiday. Music has now become background noise, listening to only when switching or working out. Sharing time with friends or relatives has become a burden that prevents you from working. Showing vulnerability is seen as a sign of weakness, and mental wellbeing remains a significant stigma. While we blame external conditions and chaos, ultimately, we are responsible for our own choices. We are human beings, not human deeds – men who owe it to us to experience the size, scope, height, and depth of life.

2. THEY ENGAGE IN PERSPECTIVE-TAKING

Getting the skills – and the ability – to walk a mile in someone else's shoes is a practice worth wearing. But seeing the world through a lens of diverse points of view – particularly those different from your own – is not easy. Patience and practice are needed. This requires putting time in understanding other people's worldviews, motives, goals, and emotions. Research documents have clear benefits. Perspective-taking has repeatedly been reported to reduce prejudice and stereotyping. Evidence also suggests that prospect-taking can make teams more creative, which can lead to better decision-making outcomes that are much needed in a complex, fast-paced world. Great people are often accustomed to enrich their perceptions of customers and employees, navigate diversity, and solve disputes through perspectives.

Imagining the future from another point of view also helps in negotiations. For example, aggressive negotiators who have a winning-take-all attitude can see their opponent as a nemesis. Perspective-taking teaches you that rivals are just individuals with their own desires. Like you, they 're passionate, shrewd, and fairly rational — they probably see you as a nemesis. In these cases, reminding yourself that you can manage your own emotions, but not your opponents is a useful first step.

Moreover, an active view of the situation from the point of view of the other person has been shown to help negotiators see, appreciate, and capitalize on these different interests to grow the pie. Outlook also allows negotiators to obtain a higher proportion of the pie.

3. THEY ARE GUIDED BY CURIOSITY

Curiosity is a powerful emotion. When you're curious, you 're more likely to venture outside your comfort zone and away from old habits. You 're more likely to think creatively and collaborate in creative ways with others. We all like to believe that we are inclusive and open to new ideas, but in fact, we are still resistant to change. The trial and evaluation process is most effective when people are open to change. The art of learning or understanding something differently involves a qualified habit of being curious, something that I discuss in my book Alive at Work: The Neuroscience of Helping Your People Enjoy What They Do.

Literature shows that framing change as a chance to explore and learn is crucial to trigger the right emotions. If you view a job as a success situation – "I have to do well or face a backlash" – it causes fear, and you are risk-averse. When you set up the same job as a learning scenario, "I wonder what I'm going to discover! "It sparks interest, and you become bolder and more determined. What's more, if you view a mission as a chance to either succeed or fail, you'll end up learning less because you're engaged in less experimentation. That, on the other hand, makes formulating new tactics challenging, because you are more likely to fall back on old tried and tested behaviors.

How can you become more curious about that? Experimental safe zones build intrinsic incentives that are far more important than extrinsic motives because they stimulate innovation. Instead of working hard, say, for fear of losing your (extrinsic) career, be fueled by your own (intrinsic) passion and curiosity. Instead of being cynical at first, be willing to explore and move experiments forward.

4. THEY NUDGE FOR GOOD

Either or not they deliberately select a position, managers in organizations are inadvertent architects of the decision-making of their employees. Each choice they make has a knock-on effect. From supporting pension contributions to setting automatic enrolment as normal to promoting healthier choices by placing healthy food at eye level at the start of the cafeteria line, companies are pushing their workers and directing them in their everyday decision-making.

Highly successful people are accustomed to behave well; they are the builder of choice intentionally. These leaders embrace the fact that even the simplest triggers in a decision-making context will distort people's choices in one direction or another. For example, we know from my own research that was merely asking for a signature at the beginning of the expense form – rather than the end – facilitates accurate reporting of expenses. Prompting a signature at the beginning of the type brings moral values sharply into focus when it matters most, encouraging accurate coverage.

Signing first is one of the strategies that demonstrate how only the most subtle of nudges can have an impact on actions and generate a ripple effect of far greater financial and ethical significance. Nudge techniques are easily convincing because they're subtle. Such limited stimuli do not limit the freedom of choice for individuals, but they may have a significant effect on critical behaviors. Managers should use nudges as tools to influence long-term success outcomes, by fostering greater coordination between policy and day-to-day operations – and by fostering a culture of honesty.

5. THEY MOVE FIRST IN NEGOTIATIONS

Life requires discussions on a regular basis. Buying a car, manipulating at work, or discussing who does the dishes: bargaining is how we get things done. In order to be more successful in these negotiations, people may want to develop a habit of making the first offer. It runs counter to the common idea that you should be waiting for the other side to talk first. Some claim that you gain insight into your counterpart and useful extra time to improve your negotiating advantage. Waiting may make sense intuitively, but research shows that, more often than not, first offers yield better outcomes.

Why? Why? First offers have a strong anchoring effect. Nobel laureate Daniel Kahneman has demonstrated a human propensity that people rely heavily on the first piece of knowledge they find, such as a quantitative calculation – an anchor. Once people receive an initial offer, they shift their own decision toward that offer. Only experts are not resistant to a strong anchoring effect. In one report, my colleagues and I had customers approach German mechanics with used cars needing repairs. After giving their own opinion on the worth of the vehicle, the customers asked the mechanics for an estimate.

Half of the mechanics had a weak anchor, with the customer recommending that the car would be sold for about DM 2,800. The other mechanics had a high anchor, around DM 5,000. The mechanics calculated that the car was worth DM 1,000 more when the anchor was set high, showing that even the expert 's decision could be subject to distortions of the mind. But watch out: highly successful people know when and when not to make the first bid. When you're in a new situation, and there are so many unknowns − when you just don't know − hang on fast, and wait for the other party to make the first move.

6. THEY FOCUS ENERGY ON WHAT MATTERS

Throughout my career, I've met several highly successful executives. Due to constant pressure to perform well, these high-fliers reach their objectives but bizarrely pile on more and more pressure. Good people set extremely high expectations for themselves, and they 're better critics than any boss. And there is a curious phenomenon: once they have achieved their version of success − wealth, rank, power − happiness does not always follow.

What's success? Sometimes, when you dig down, you realize that success comes from happiness. Highly successful people are really content people. The common trait of highly productive individuals is the ability to concentrate time and energy on things that matter. Let's do a short exercise: what are your top priorities? Go on, write it down. Now, look at your journal for the last three months. How much time did you spend working through them? Generally, the reaction is: not nearly enough. Many chief executives agree that they invest as little as 1% of their time on issues that will drive the potential success of the company. It may feel too busy to concentrate on what's important.

The defensive wall between work and life has broken – employment has now blended into life. Stress leads to loss of control – at home and at work – and we waste so much time on inconsequential issues and interests that render us indifferent or dispassionate. Therefore, very productive people have the potential to be ruthless with their time. Every day, they ask, "I spend my time and energy on matters?

7. THEY CHERISH CREATIVITY AND THINK DIFFERENTLY

Some of the business habits are harmful: chief executives can get high on the stale air of sycophancy. CFOs may not always know when to stop the organization's extreme, cost-reducing diet, failing to see that the corporate body needs no more slimming. And, if not kept in check, well-intentioned CTOs can snore words like digitization, blockchain, or cyber just too often for their own sake. We already know that, without them, we are heading aimlessly, cloudlessly to a world called disruption, from where we, the dinosaurs, will never return.

These are all ugly habits. In my view, however, no practice is more deadly than the tolerance of negativity. When culture eats breakfast strategy, cynicism kills culture for sport. Unlike drugs, depression can sound euphoric at the moment, but over time it sneezes the senses and causes immense harm at massive doses.

I also ask executives to share recent experiences with the killer of this toxic society. Definitions vary from the blunt—"We really don't have time for this"—to the bizarre—"I know this concept is untested, so why can't you promise it's going to make money before we evaluate it? Creativity is the good behavior of a successful leader.

Not the mere domain of the crazies in the marketing or engineering divisions. Creativity is good for personal and social well-being and is our most powerful friend as we face new situations and issues we have never seen before (or too frequently seen).

PARADIGM SHIFTS

During my 50 years as a worldwide macro investor, I find it very long periods (about ten years), in which markets and relationships work in a way that most people adjust and extrapolate slowly, leading to shifts to new paradigms, in which markets move more in the opposite direction, rather than in the opposite direction. Identification and tactical treatment of these paradigms are important to the investor 's success (which we are trying to do through our Pure Alpha moves) and the structure of our portfolio so that we are relatively resistant (which we are trying to achieve through our All-Wetter portfolios).

HOW PARADIGM SHIFTS OCCUR

There are still huge unstable forces pushing the paradigm. They 're going on long enough for people to conclude that they're never going to stop, even though they clearly have to stop. A composite of these is the unsustainable rate of debt growth that promotes the acquisition of investment assets; it pushes up asset prices, which leads people to believe that investing and purchasing such investment assets is a good thing to do. Yet that can't go on indefinitely, as companies investing and purchasing those assets will run out of borrowing power, and debt service costs will increase compared to their revenues by amounts that compress their cash flows. There's a paradigm shift when these events happen. Debtors are being squeezed, and credit issues are emerging, and there is a decline in lending and spending on products, services, and financial properties, and they are going down in a self-reinforcing cycle that looks more contrary than the previous paradigm. It persists until it's overdone, which reverses in a way that I'm not going to fall into, which is clarified in my book Principles for Navigating Major Debt Crises, which you can get here for free.

Another classic example that comes to mind is that long stretches of low volatility appear to lead to high volatility, as people adjust to the low volatility, which causes them to do stuff (like borrowing more money than they would borrow if volatility were higher) the expose them to more volatility, resulting in a self-reinforcing volatility pick-up. There are a lot of classic examples like this that happen over time that I'm not going to get into now. Still, I would like to emphasize that knowing what types of paradigms exist and how they could be changed is required to invest well consistently. That's because any single approach to investing — e.g., investing in any type of asset class, investing in any kind of investment style (e.g., interest, growth, hardship), investing in anything — will experience a period where it performs so poorly that it can kill you. Investing in a sovereign "cash" (i.e., short debt) which can not be defaulted, which most people consider to be risk-free, is not because the cash returns to the owner are denominated in currencies, so that the central bank can "print" to be deprived in value when enough money is printed to hold interest rates well below inflation.

In paradigm changes, most people get caught over-extended, doing something too common and getting really hurt. On the other hand, if you are astute enough to consider these transitions, you will handle them well, or at least defend yourself against them. The financial crisis of 2008-09, which was the last big paradigm change, was one such time. This is because debt growth rates were unsustainable as they were before the 1929-1932 paradigm shift. Since we were looking at these days, we saw that we were heading for another "one of those," because what was happening was unsustainable, and we sailed the recession well while other investors had a battle.

I think it's a good time now to look at past paradigms and paradigm shifts, and 2) to think about the paradigm in which we are and how that might shift as we're late in the new and are likely to come close to a transition. To do this, I have written this report in two sections: first: "Paradigms and Paradigm Changes over the last 100 years;" and second: "The coming Paradigm Change." If you are able to read these two paradigms, it is advisable that you begin by "Paradigms and Paradigm Shifts during the last 100 years." There is also an appendix with more explanations for those who want to examine it more thoroughly every decade from the 1920s to the present.

PARADIGMS AND PARADIGM SHIFTS OVER THE LAST 100 YEARS

History has shown us that paradigms and paradigm shifts still occur and that it is necessary to learn and plan yourself for them as an investor and beyond. The aim of this work is to show you business and economic paradigms and their changes in the last 100 years. In the following chapter, "The Change of the Coming Paradigm," I explain my thoughts on the one before me.

Instead of limiting time and space, I shall focus only on those in the U.S. because they are sufficient to give you the insight that I would like to convey. At some point, however, I will teach you the same way I did in the Big Debt Crisis concepts to handle Big Debt Crystals because I think it is important to learn them all to understand the workings of the markets and economies timelessly and fundamentally.

HOW PARADIGMS AND PARADIGM SHIFTS WORK

As you know, market pricing is the future forecast; as such, it very clearly reflects market growth. The markets then adjust as a result of the way things happen as planned. As a result, market management needs a better-informed view of what will happen than a consensus that is incorporated into the price. It's the game. This is why it is so important to grasp these paradigms and paradigm shifts.

I have found that the view of the majority is usually more influenced by what has happened recently (i.e., in recent years), than by what is more likely to happen. It appears to presume that the paradigms that existed would continue, and it does not expect paradigm changes, which is why we have such significant consumer and economic changes. Such changes, more often than not, lead to markets and economies behaving more in the opposite direction than they did in the previous paradigm.

What follows is my explanation of paradigm changes and paradigm changes in the US over the last 100 years. It contains a combination of facts and subjective opinions, and when faced with the option of sharing these subjective thoughts or leaving them out, I felt that it was easier to include them along with this warning mark. My degree of closeness to these encounters inevitably influences the consistency of my explanations. Since my direct impressions started in the early 1960s, my perceptions of the years have been most vivid since then. Although less detailed, my knowledge of markets and economies back to the 1920s is still pretty good, both because of my extensive analysis of it and because of my interaction with the people of the generation of my parents who have witnessed it. Like in the years before the 1920s, my knowledge comes solely from researching the major market and economic trends, and it's not as good because it doesn't exist. I've been researching economic and market developments in major countries over the last year, dating back to about 1500, which has given me a shallow understanding of them. From this insight, I can honestly say that all the years I've learned the same major events happen over and over again for exactly the same reasons. I'm not suggesting that they're exactly the same or that there haven't been any big changes, because there definitely have (e.g., how central banks have gone away and changed). What I'm saying is that major paradigm changes have always happened, and they've happened for basically the same reasons.

To show them, I've divided history into decades, starting with the 1920s, because they correlate well enough with paradigm shifts to convey the picture. Although not necessarily precisely synchronized, paradigm changes coincidentally appeared to occur during decade changes — e.g., the 1920s were "roaring," the 1930s were in "depression," the 1970s were stimulative, the 1980s were disinflationary, etc. Even, I believe that we're looking at

Ten-year time horizons allow us to put things in perspective. It's also a nice coincidence that we're in the last months of this decade, so it's a fun exercise to start imagining what the next decade of the '20s would be like, which is my target, rather than concentrate on exactly what's going to happen in a quarter or a year.

Until briefly discussing each of these decades, I would like to make a few points that you can watch out for as we discuss each of them.

✓ Through decade had its own distinctive attributes, but there were long-lasting stretches (e.g., 1 to 3 years) that had almost the exact opposite characteristics to what was typical of the decade. To successfully deal with these shifts, one would have had to complete the ins and outs effectively, or fade the moves (i.e., buy more when prices fell and sell more when prices rose), or have a healthy portfolio that would have stayed fairly stable through the moves. The wrong thing would have been to switch (sell after price decreases and purchase after price increases).

✓ The global economic and market movements have been undulating in broad swings due to the sequence of actions and reactions of policymakers, investors, business owners, and staff. In the cycle of over-growing economic conditions and stock valuations, the seeds of reversals germinated. For example, the very debt that funded excesses in economic activity and commodity prices generated commitments that could not be fulfilled, which led to the decline. Likewise, the more severe economic conditions were the stronger the policymakers' responses to reverse them were. Among these reasons, we've seen significant economic and financial swings around "equilibrium" rates over the last decades.

✓ By the end of each decade, most investors expected the next decade to be identical to the previous decade, but due to the cycle of excesses leading to excesses and undulations mentioned above, the decades that followed were more opposite than the decades that preceded them. As a result, market fluctuations due to these paradigm changes were usually very large and unpredictable, triggering significant shifts in income.

✓ Every major asset class had great and terrible decades, so much so that any investor who had invested much of their money in any one investment would have lost almost all of it at one time or another.

✓ Ideas on how to spend always shifted, generally to justify how they made sense in the last few years, and when they didn't make sense. Such backward-looking theories were usually the best at the end of the paradigm era and proved to be horrible investment guides in the next decade, making them very harmful. That's why it's so important to see the full spectrum of past paradigms and paradigm shifts and to plan one's investment strategy so that it can work well through them all. The worst thing that can be done, particularly late in the process, is to construct one's portfolio based on what should have performed well in the past ten years, but that's normal.

It's for these reasons that we're investing the way we do — i.e., that's why we've developed a balanced All Weather portfolio that's structured to stay fairly steady while high, well-diversified, and developed a Pure Alpha portfolio to make tactical timing moves.

HOW TO SHIFT PARADIGMS

The knowledge you've just gained is going to change your life in amazing ways — if you take action.

However, before you get going, there are a few things you need to be sure about.

Next, note that the concept is a multitude of patterns in the subconscious mind.

Second, you need to change the paradigm in the same way that it was created — through the repetition of knowledge.

And, thirdly, you must realize that in order to shift a pattern, you must deliberately and actively substitute an "evil" habit with a positive habit. Otherwise, you 're going to make another bad habit, because nature abhors a vacuum.

Start the cycle by deliberately selecting new beliefs that are consistent with the patterns you like, and then plant them in your subconscious mind instead of the old beliefs.

One way to do so is by assumptions. Find positive statements that represent your values or actions and read the statements over and over again. If you want more money, you can use the statement that I shared with you in the video.

I am so pleased and thankful that money is coming to me in rising quantities from various sources on a continuous basis.

One important technique you can use is visioning, which is where you create a new picture of yourself becoming, doing, or doing the things you want. This master is Sandy! This practice several times a day allows you to break bad habits and put into your life the things you want.

You may also do the following exercise:

Think of the outcome that you're having that you don't like, and ask yourself what behaviors or habits the outcome is creating.

Write out the actions in perfectly clear detail.

Tell yourself whose pattern or action is the complete opposite of the action you've just described.

Write a new action on another sheet of paper.

Burn the document that has a bad habit (as a symbolic gesture).

Write out a good practice four or five times a day. Read this regularly. Eventually, you can lodge the idea in your subconscious mind.

Once it begins to take hold, it takes power away from a bad habit, and the bad habit eventually dies from a lack of nutrition. Then the one who has been deposited takes over.

Now it's going to take a fair amount of energy and knowledge to do this stuff, but I promise you, it's going to be worth a lot of effort, because it's going to allow you to write your own ticket in life.

As I changed my mindset, my life changed literally like night and day.

HOW HABITS WORK

The challenge in researching the science of habits is that most people want to know the mysterious formula easily if they get to know this field of research. If scientists have discovered how these trends work, then the explanation is that they must have also found a blueprint for rapid change, right?

If it was just that fast.

It's not like there are no rules. The challenge is that there is not a single strategy for changing behaviors. There are thousands of them.

Individuals and behaviors are all different, and so the nuances of diagnosing and modifying patterns in our lives vary from individual to individual and behavior to behavior. Giving up cigarettes is different from curbing overeating, which is different from improving how you interact with your partner, which is different from how you approach work. What's more, the behaviors of each person are guided by various desires.

As a consequence, this book does not contain a single prescription. Rather, I was hoping to offer something else: a structure for understanding how behaviors work, and a guide to experimenting with how they could change. Some patterns are easy to examine and affect. Others are more nuanced and obstinate, requiring prolonged analysis. And for some, a transition is a process that never comes to a complete conclusion.

Yet that doesn't mean it can't happen. Each chapter of this book discusses a specific aspect of why habits occur and how they work. The method outlined in this appendix is an effort to distill, in a very simple way, the techniques that researchers have used to diagnose and form patterns in our own lives. It is not intended to be detailed. It's just a practical guide, a place to start. And combined with deeper lessons from the chapters of this book, it's a roadmap for where to go next.

The transition might not be fast, and it's not always easy. But with time and commitment, almost any pattern can be reshaped.

IDENTIFY THE ROUTINE

I found a basic neural loop at the heart of any behavior. A loop made up of three parts: a prompt, a routine, and a reward.

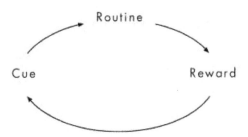

To understand your own patterns, you need to identify the components of your loops. After a pattern cycle has been established with a specific behavior, you should find ways to substitute old vices with new habits.

As an example, let us say that you are unusual to go to the cafeteria and buy a chocolate chip cookie every afternoon, as I did when I began to research this book. Let's claim that this habit helped you gain a couple of pounds. Actually, let's say you got exactly 8 pounds from this practice, and your wife made some pointed remarks. You wanted to resist – you even went so far as to put a message on your computer reading "NO MORE COOKIES."

But you get to forget the message every afternoon, run around the cafeteria, buy a cookie and eat it in conversation with colleagues in the cash register. It's good, and it's bad. You tell yourself tomorrow that you're going to have the courage to fight. It's going to be different tomorrow.

But the habit comes again tomorrow. How do you begin to diagnose and then change your behavior? By finding the pattern loop. The first step is the routine definition. In this case of cookies, repeating, as with most behaviors, is the most obvious aspect: it is the behavior you would like to improve. Your routine is to get up in the evening from your desk, go to the cafeteria, buy a chocolate chip cookie, and enjoy it with your colleagues. And that's what you put in the loop, exactly:

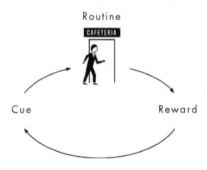

First, a few less straightforward questions: what is this routine's secret? Is it hunger? Abortion? Abortion? Low sugar in the blood, huh? Because before you get into another mission, you need a break?

And what's the reward for you?

The cookie alone?

The change in scenery, huh?

A short distraction, huh? Socialize with friends, right? And the explosion of energy from the explosion of sugar?

To do this, you may need to do a little work.

EXPERIMENT WITH REWARDS

The rewards are important when they meet their desires. But we often do not know about the hunger that drives our acts. When the marketing department of Febreze found that customers required a fresh fragrance, for example, at the end of a cleaning routine, they found that none knew that there was no one. It's hidden insight. Some cravings are like this: clear in retrospect, but painfully hard to see while under their influence.

To find out what cravings drive specific behaviors, experimenting with different incentives is helpful. It might take a few days, a week, or longer. At that point, you shouldn't feel any pressure to make any real change – think of yourself as a data collection scientist.

When you feel like you are going to the cafeteria to buy a cookie on the first day of your experiment, change your routine to make another incentive for you. For instance, go out and walk around the block instead of going to a cafeteria, and then return to your desk without eating anything. The following day, go to the café to buy a donut or a candy bar and enjoy it on site. Go to the cafeteria the next day, buy and eat the apple as you talk to your colleagues. Instead, have a cup of coffee. So instead of going to a restaurant, just go back to the office of your friend and talk for a few minutes.

You get the picture. What you want to do instead of buying a cookie is not important. It's a matter of testing different theories to decide which addiction is driving your routine. Are you looking for a treat on your own or a break from work? If this is a cookie, is it because you're hungry? (In which case the

61

apple would perform just as well.) Or is it that you want the strength of the cookie to burst? (And then the coffee will be enough.) Or are you walking up to the cafeteria as an excuse to socialize, and the cookie is only a convenient excuse? (If so, going to someone's office and snorkeling for a few minutes would fulfill the urge.)

When you check four or five different incentives, you can use an old trick to search for patterns: for each task, place the first three items on a piece of paper that come to mind when you get back to your office. These can be feelings, random thoughts, observations of how you feel, or even the first three words that pop into your mind.

Then set the alarm on your watch or your machine for 15 minutes. So soon as it goes off, ask yourself: do you always have the desire for a cookie?

The explanation of why it's important to write down three items – even if they're empty words – is twofold. Second, it induces a momentary perception of what you think or feel. Much like Mandy, the nail biter held a note card filled with hash marks to compel her to become conscious of her normal impulses and writing three words demands a moment of focus. What're more, studies show that writing down a few words helps you recall what you were feeling at the moment. At the end of the experiment, it would be much easier to recall what you think and felt at that particular moment as you study your notes because the scribbled words would evoke a wave of recollection.

So why the warning of 15 minutes? Since the point of these assessments is to assess the incentive you 're looking for. Unless you still want to get up and go to the cafeteria, fifteen minutes after eating a donut, the habits are not driven by sugar addiction. When you still want a cookie after going to the office of a friend, then the need for human contact is not what determines your actions.

On the other side, if 15 minutes after talking to a buddy, you consider it simple to get back to work, then you've found the reward — temporary diversion and socialization — that your habit was trying to fulfill.

By playing with various incentives, you will separate what you really want, which is key to reshaping your habit.

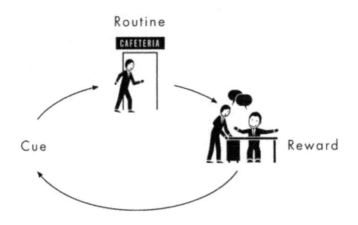

When you've worked out the pattern and incentive, what's left is to identify the cue.

ISOLATE THE CUE

Around a decade ago, a psychologist at the University of Western Ontario sought to address a query that had been perplexed by social scientists for years: why do certain crime eyewitnesses misremember what they see, while others interpret incidents accurately?

In addition, the recollections of eyewitnesses are extremely significant. But studies suggest that eyewitnesses frequently misremember what they hear. We insist that the perpetrator was a male, for example, because she was wearing a skirt; or that the crime occurred at noon, even though police reports claim it happened at 2:00 p.m. Many eyewitnesses, on the other hand, will remember the incidents they witnessed with almost complete recall.

Dozens of research have looked at this phenomenon, seeking to establish why certain individuals are better eyewitnesses than others. Studies have suggested that certain people actually have stronger memory, or that a crime that happens in a familiar location is easier to recall. Yet such hypotheses were not checked − people with good and poor memory, or more and less familiar with the crime scene, were equally likely to misremember what had happened.

The psychologist at the University of Western Ontario has taken a new approach. He wondered if the researchers were making a mistake by concentrating on what the questioners and the witnesses said, rather than how they said it. He believed that there were implicit signals that affected the questioning process. Yet as she watched the videotape of the witness interviews, searching for certain answers, she couldn't see anything. There was so much movement in each interview – all the facial gestures, the various ways in which the questions were asked, the fluctuating emotions – that she did not identify any patterns.

And she came up with an idea: she made a list of a few things that she would concentrate on – the sound of the questioners, the facial expressions of the witness, and how similar the witness and the questioner were to each other. Instead, she eliminated any details that could distract her from those elements. She turned the volume down on the TV, so instead of hearing words, all she could see was the sound of the questioner's voice. She placed a sheet of paper over the questioner's ear so that she could see the testimony of the witnesses. She placed a tape measure on the monitors to measure their distance from each other.

And as soon as she started researching these basic elements, the patterns jumped out. She saw that witnesses who misremembered the facts were typically confronted by cops who used a soft, polite tone. If the witnesses smiled more or stood closer to the questioner, they were more likely to misremember.

In other words, when environmental stimuli said, "we are friends" – a soothing tone, a smiling face – the witnesses were more likely to misremember what had happened. It may have been because, subconsciously, the friendship cues caused a pattern of satisfying the questioner.

Yet, the significance of this experiment is that hundreds of other researchers have observed the same recordings. A lot of smart people had seen the same trends, but no one had ever noticed them before. Even in each tape, there was too much detail to see a clear warning.

But, as soon as the psychologist decided to focus on only three categories of actions and remove the extraneous information, the patterns jumped out.

Our lives are the same thing. The reason why it's so hard to recognize the signals that stimulate our behaviors is that there's so much information to bomb us as our behavior unfolds. Tell yourself, do you have breakfast every day at a certain time because you're hungry?

Or because the clock says 7:30 a.m.? Perhaps because your children have begun to eat? Maybe because you're dressed, and that's when the breakfast routine starts?

When you shut your car off automatically when driving to work, what causes the behavior? A sign on the street? A particular tree, huh? Understanding that this is the right route? Are they all together? If you're driving your kid to school, and you find that you've started taking the path to work, rather than to school, abstinently, what caused the mistake? What was the signal that triggered the 'drive to work' habit to kick in instead of the 'drive to school' pattern?

To locate the signal in the midst of the chaos, we should use the same method as the psychologist: Locate types of habits that need to be tested in advance to see trends. Luckily, science is providing some support in this regard. Experiments have shown that almost all the normal cues fall into one of the five categories:

✓ Location

✓ Time

✓ Emotional State

✓ Other People

✓ Immediately preceding action

So, if you're trying to find out the trigger for 'going to the cafeteria and buying a chocolate chip cookie' habit, you write down five items when the impulse hits (these were my specific notes when I was trying to treat my habit):

✓ Where are you now? (Sit at my desk)

✓ What time is it? (3:36 p.m.)

✓ What is your mental state? (bored) as well

✓ Who else is around? (No one at all)

✓ Which action was followed by the urge? (Answered by email)

The next day:

✓ Where are you now? (walking back from the copying machine)

✓ What time is it? (3:18 p.m.)

✓ What is your mental state? (Happily)

✓ Who else is around? (Jim of the Sports)

✓ Which action was followed by the urge? (Made a photocopy of it)

The third day:

✓ Where are you now? (Meeting room)

✓ What time is it? (3:41 p.m.)

✓ What is your mental state? (I 'm tired, excited about the project I 'm working on)

✓ Who else is around? (The editors who are coming to this meeting)

✓ Which action was followed by the urge? (I was sitting because the meeting was about to begin)

Three days in, it was pretty obvious what kind of signal would cause my cookie habit – I felt the urge to have a snack at some point in the day. I had already learned in step two that my conduct was not motivated by hunger. The reward I was looking for was a brief diversion – the kind that comes from gossip with a friend. And the habit, I realized now, was activated between 3:00 and 4:00 a.m.

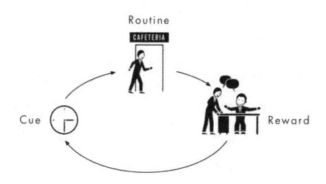

HAVE A PLAN

When you've worked out the pattern loop – you've established the reward that activates the behavior, the signal that causes it, and the routine itself – you can start modifying your behavior. You can move to a better routine by preparing for the cue and selecting an action that provides the reward you 're looking for. What you need here is a strategy.

During the prolog, we learned that a habit is a choice that we consciously make at some point, and then avoid thinking about, but continue to do so, sometimes every day.

In another way, the habit is the rule that our brain follows automatically: when I see CUE, I 'm going to do ROUTINE to get a REWARD.

To re-engineer the process, we need to start making choices again. And, according to study after study, the best way to do so is to have a strategy. In the world of psychology, such proposals are known as 'implementation goals.'

Take my cookie-in-the-afternoon habit, for example. Through using this method, I discovered that it was around 3:30 a.m. in the afternoon. I figured my routine was going to the cafeteria, buying a cookie, and talking to friends. And, through experimenting, I've found that it wasn't just the cookie I wanted – it was a moment of relaxation and a chance to socialize.

So, I was writing a plan:

Around 3:30 a.m., every day, I'm going to walk to a friend's office and chat for 10 minutes.

Just make sure I was doing this, I set the alarm on my watch at 3:30 a.m.

It didn't work right away. There were days when I was too distracted and ignored the alarm, and then I fell off the wagon. At other times, it seemed like too much hassle to find a friend willing to talk – it was easier to get a cookie, and so I gave in to the temptation. Yet the day I implemented my strategy – when my alarm went off, I forced myself to walk to a friend's office and talk for 10 minutes – I found that I finished my workday feeling happier. I didn't go to the kitchen, I didn't eat a cookie, so I felt great. Finally, it was automatic: when the alarm rang, I found a friend and finished the day feeling a slight but real sense of accomplishment. For a few weeks, I didn't care about the routine anymore. So when I couldn't find someone to talk with, I went to the cafeteria, so I bought tea and drank it with my parents.

This all happened about six months ago. I don't have my watch anymore. I lost it at some point. Yet at around 3:30 a.m. every day, I get up, look around the newsroom for someone to talk to, spend 10 minutes talking about the news, and then go back to my office. This happens even without me knowing about it. It's been a habit.

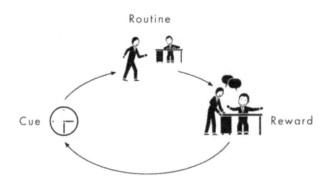

Obviously, certain patterns can be more difficult to alter. Yet this structure is a starting point. Often it takes a long time to adjust. It also involves repeated tests and failures. But once you understand how the pattern works – once you identify the trigger, the routine, and the incentive – you gain control over it.

HOW TO CREATE NEW HABIT

How long does it take to build a new habit?

The time period can vary from one second to several years. The pace of the development of the new pattern of behavior is largely dictated by the strength of the emotion that follows the decision to start behaving in a specific way.

A lot of people dream, talk about and plan to lose weight and become physically fit. It could go on for years. So one day, the doctor says, "If you don't lose weight and improve your physical health, you 're in danger of dying at an early age."

Immediately, the thought of dying can be so overwhelming or terrifying that the individual suddenly changes his or her diet, starts to exercise, avoids smoking, and becomes a healthy, active person. Psychologists refer to this as an "important emotional experience." Any experience of extreme happiness or pain, combined with actions, will create a regular pattern of behavior that will continue for the rest of a person's life.

For example, placing your hand on a hot stove or touching a live electrical wire will cause you severe, immediate pain or shock. Training will only take a split second. Yet for the rest of your life, you 're going to have a habit of not putting your hand on hot stoves or touching live electrical wires. The habit would have been developed immediately and would have continued forever. It might come as a shock to you to learn that at the beginning of the 20th Century, hardly anyone brushed their teeth; in fact, so many soldiers had rotting teeth during World War I that government officials considered bad dental hygiene a national security risk. It all changed, however, when a marketing genius named Claude Hopkins was convinced by an old acquaintance to apply his talents to hawking toothpaste.

Claude was responsible for taking obscure items like Goodyear and Quaker Oats and transforming them into household names. His signature strategies were to tap into the habit loop by anchoring the product to a particular trigger, irrespective of how preposterous the link was. Quaker Oats, for example, owes its popularity to Claude's ability to persuade America that he had 24-hour energy – but only if you eat a bowl every morning.

Claude chose a similar guide to transform toothpaste into a national habit. His advertising says, "Just run your tongue through your teeth. You 're going to feel a film – that's what makes your teeth look 'off-color' and it's calling for decay.

"After giving people the cue, he continued with pictures of perfect white smiles and a quote," Notice how many pretty teeth you see everywhere. Millions of people are using a modern form of teeth brushing. Why would a woman have a dingy movie on her teeth? Pepsodent is removing the video! The assertion was quite false; the "film" is a naturally occurring membrane, and the toothpaste does nothing to remove it. Nevertheless, the cue was universal and easy to see, and people bought a link to the reward (beautiful teeth). In a decade, toothpaste use had risen from 7% of the population to 65%. The author compares this success with the abject failure of P&G's Febreze when it first came onto the market.

This was a true scientific marvel that worked like a charm; the issue was the nature of the human olfactory system that causes people to become accustomed to any scent and to lose their ability to detect this. The lady with nine cats and a house scent of matching did not have enough cue to persuade her to use the drug that would possibly change her social life. P&G executives were on the verge of axing the drug when the product management team learned what scientists already knew: that a habit is created only when the brain starts to predict and expect rewards when the stimulus is applied before the routine is completed.

You can't market a commodity that offers fragrancelessness because there's no way the brain can foresee it. The sales of Febreze shot through the roof as soon as P&G started promoting the drug as an air freshener – a product to be used as the final phase in the cleaning process to make the space comfortably aromatic. Once people tried the drug, they started to love the clean scent of the finished spritz of Febreze. Much later did P&G begin to mention the true significance of the drug – a revolutionary chemical solution that completely removes odors, rather than only covering them up. It is here where the writers have revealed that the methods of Claude Hopkins have had little effect on the selling of Pepsodent toothpaste. A lot of other toothpaste firms used similar methods even before Pepsodent came along. In fact, the success of that particular toothpaste was completely accidental.

By anticipating the impact of the option, Pepsodent had included citric acid, mint oil, and other ingredients that had created the now-familiar cool, tingling effect. The feeling made the cue – people skipped the feeling when they forgot to brush their teeth. The tingling has no other meaning than to let people know that the product is working. (The foam in today's tooth paste is equally unnecessary from a practical point of view)

How long does it take to form a habit?

It takes some 21 days, according to the experts, to break or shape a habit pattern of medium complexity. Habits that are difficult or more complicated to assimilate into your way of life may take longer.

Break a habit or make a habit in 21 days

Three weeks might not seem like a very long time, but you're going to develop good habits within 21 days.

This is simple habits, like waking up early at a certain hour, practicing a day before you start, listening to podcasts in your car, going to bed at a certain hour, getting ready for appointments in advance, prepared for your day, beginning with your most important tasks every day, or finishing your tasks before you start anything else.

These are medium complexity patterns that can be easily established in 14-21 days by practice and repetition.

Focus on One New Habit

If you are to learn how to make a new habit, ego depletion, and how it holds you down are the main thing that you need to consider.

Ego depletion is "an individual's decreased ability to control emotions, feelings, and actions."

This affects our ability to develop new behaviors, as our willpower supply is distributed across all aspects of our lives.

It is important, therefore, to concentrate on only one habit at a time. Thus, your willpower can be channeled to the one habit and to the chances of success.

And the question is this:

"What new habits would you like to make? Identify it now, and read what you can do right.

Become an expert in this practice and dig deeply into all material that is important for getting started.

That's something that I do every day, so I'm still working hard to improve it on a regular basis. I'm trying to define a routine, something that mixes with your life and can't be done regularly, even if you don't feel like it.

Because of ego depletion, focusing on only one habit at a time is important.

Thus, your store of willpower can be turned into one habit, and the chances of success can be increased.

Form a new habit? Commit for a MINIMUM of 21 days.

Some people say it takes 21 days to develop a habit, while others say it takes 66 days. The reality is that the amount of time always varies from person to person and from habit to habit. You may find that some behaviors are easy to create, while others take more effort. My recommendation is to stick to a new pattern for the next 30 days (or one month to keep it simple).

At this time, your entire life will be organized around carving out time every day to be consistent.

Anchor Your New Habit to an Established Habit

A habit should not be based on inspiration, fads, or a fleeting urge. Actually, it should be instilled in your life to the point that it becomes commonplace. It also means that you don't need a complex collection of steps — just something that you can stick to day in and day out — forever.

All you want to do is stick to a very small change of habit and take baby steps while you build on it. A significant aspect of his teaching is to "anchor" the new practice of what you already do on a daily basis.

- ✓ "After I get out of work at my house, I'm going to change my workout clothes and walk for 10 minutes."

- ✓ "After brushing my teeth at night, I'm going to write down everything I've eaten for the day."

- ✓ "When I drop off my kids at the babysitter, I'm going to stop at the gym for my yoga class."

You 're getting the picture. Just consider a pattern that you already regularly do, and then reinforce it with a new action.

Take Baby Steps

The disadvantage of relying on inspiration alone to build a new habit is that you don't have a contingency plan when you're not in the mood. Basically, the only way to make a habit stick is to turn it into an unconscious action. You can achieve so by taking small steps and by building a low degree of commitment.

The aim here is to build a micro-commitment where it is difficult to fail. It is more important to be consistent and not to miss a day than to reach a particular milestone. What you're going to find is that when you have a low level of dedication, you 're more likely to get started.

Examples of zeroing on a micro-commitment include:

- ✓ walking for just five minutes a day.

- ✓ Writing a paragraph about your book.

- ✓ Eat one helping of vegetables every day.

- ✓ Making a sales call to a prospective client.

- ✓ Waking up 10 minutes earlier every morning.

The trick to habit growth is to make micro-commitments and concentrate on small wins. Build a micro-commitment where it is difficult to lose.

Odds are, these things seem to be too basic. And that's why they're so good!

You want to devote yourself to something so simple that it's difficult to miss a day. So, when you get started, you're always going to do more than you expected.

Make a Plan for Obstacles

Each new habit is going to have obstacles. A significant portion of the DGH platform is devoted to working through the stumbling blocks of your progress. Once you know in advance, what the challenges are, you will take proactive steps to overcome them.

Examples of may barriers:

✓ Time

✓ Pain

✓ Weather

✓ Space

✓ Costs

✓ Self-consciousness

Prepare for these challenges and know that they will arrive. Then you're not going to blindside them. This goes back to the "If-Then Preparation" we were talking about. Examples of these strong "If-Then" statements include:

✓ "When I check the weather, and it's raining, I'm going to work out at the gym instead."

✓ "If I don't have time for my project at the end of the day, I'll continue to wake up for 30 minutes and work on it before anything else."

✓ "When I have a particularly rough day at work, and I don't feel like working out, I'm still going to exercise easily for at least 15 minutes."

Create Accountability for Your Habit

Track your efforts and make public announcements about your new habit. In light of the lessons learned from the Hawthorne effect, you are more likely to follow through with dedication while you are being watched by others. To stick with this new routine, you need to let others know about your efforts and goals.

Post updates to social media pages, use applications like Chains, and Coach.me to monitor your progress, collaborate with an accountability partner, or post daily updates to an online community related to your behaviors. Do whatever it takes to get encouragement from others to help the daily routine.

Never underestimate the influence of mutual consent. Just realizing that you're going to be kept responsible for your behavior keeps you focused and consistent.

Important Reward Milestones

There's no reason for a new habit of being dull. Work on building a reward program in the process so that you can take time to celebrate the successful achievement of your goals. The reward you get is up to you, but it's important to enjoy those great moments along the way.

Bear in mind, and there's no need for a payout to split the bank. You may want to check out a new movie, enjoy a night out with your significant other, or just do something you love.

We continue to underestimate the importance of having fun when developing habits. Sometimes, however, having a simple incentive for consistently performing an action will help you stick to a new routine.

Work on building a reward program in the process so that you can take time to celebrate the successful achievement of your goals.

Build a New Identity

Repeating a habit on a regular basis is only going to get you so far. You can do a lot by committing yourself to a small step, doing it every day, through the commitment over time, and overcoming obstacles.

Yet, at some point, you need to go from just doing it every day to making it part of your core identity. Only then can you stick to it without the overwhelming need for reinforcement.

James Clear also speaks about what he's called Identity-Based Habits. The hope here is that you can create a long-lasting habit by making it a representation of who you are inside.

Simply put, you need to believe the habit is part of what makes you a special person.

He points out that most goals (and habits) are based on a particular result (such as achieving a specific amount of income or receiving industry-relevant accolades).

It's easier to accept that the habit is just part of your personality, and then use any "small victory" as a way to show that you're inside.

It always starts with a change of mind.

For a new habit, strengthen that practice by saying things like, "I am the type of person who consistently likes the type of workout." Instead, follow through by doing it on a daily basis.

Finally, this day-to-day routine will suit your internal identity.

HOW THE WILLPOWER BECOMES AUTOMATIC

For several years, scientists have known that willpower is a crucial component to success, even more than intelligence. In a successful Stanford study in the 1960s, researchers sat four-year-olds at a table with a single marshmallow and told them they could either eat it immediately or wait for the researcher to come back 15 minutes later and win an extra marshmallow.

Researchers then studied the children while they were in high school, and noticed that those who could retain self-control long enough to win two marshmallows as four-year-olds now had higher grades, SAT scores, and social achievement. (The book The Marshmallow Test is titled, based on this experiment, and is a great one to read.)

We do know that both of us have a finite supply of willpower. In a case western study in the 1990s, researchers advised a group of undergraduate students to miss a meal and then sit down together, each in front of two bowls. One bowl featured new, delicious chocolate chip cookies, while the other contained slightly less appetizing radishes. Half were told to eat only the cookies, and the rest were told to eat only the radishes. The researchers then presented the students with a difficult puzzle to solve.

None of the students realized the puzzle was difficult, but the students who had just eaten the radishes gave up much faster than the students who had just eaten the cookies – an average of eight minutes, compared to 19 minutes of perseverance for the cookie eaters. This 60% difference was triggered by the loss of the will of the radish eaters as they had to avoid sweets. (That's why, in the morning, you don't want to waste your will on tiresome, unimportant things like writing emails.)

In addition, multiple studies have shown that by practicing willpower in one field, such as exercise or schooling, you can increase your reserve of willpower and be able to extend it to other areas of life. None of these things, however, is enough to exercise adequate willpower reliably.

The secret is something that was central to the success of the Starbucks coffee chain: the methodical preparation of routines for those inflections where pain and temptation are the greatest.

Starbucks' training programs direct workers through the detection of inflection points (such as when an unhappy customer is shouting at the wrong drink) and the alignment of the inflection point to one of the company's hundreds of procedures. Through selecting a certain action ahead of time, discipline becomes a routine, and workers are able to deliver a high level of service that keeps consumers coming back for expensive lattes.

Another secret to Starbucks' success is how the organization allows staff to use their own intelligence and imagination. In research at the University of Albany, students were put in front of a cookie tray.

The researchers kindly asked half of the students not to eat cookies, explained the intent of the experiment to them, and thanked them for contributing their time. The researchers told the other half not to eat cookies without specifying or thanking the purpose of the experiment. Afterward, the first party substantially outperformed the second in an unrelated standard computerized concentration test.

Although scientists do not yet completely understand the mechanisms of the cycle, it is clear that people perform much better and have much greater willpower when they feel like what they do is a personal decision, and when they understand the intent. When people only obey orders, the force of will is even more difficult.

Voluntary control is the main habit in Starbucks' approach to training. Many research tends to recognize willpower/self-control/self-discipline as the single most significant keystone behavior for individual success. Longitudinal research measuring children's determination, and then continuing to monitor their lives, consistently show a high correlation between those who resisted and those who were chosen for sought after schools and received higher SATs. Self-discipline has a greater effect on academic success than IQ. So force yourself to make willpower a habit. Starbucks is now teaching self-discipline to enhance service efficiency. Willpower can be taught.

Researcher Mark Muraven was not happy with the definition of willpower as an ability. Knowledge is something that is normally gained and not lost, so why does it appear to ebb and flow? He has shown that willpower is finite. Like a muscle, if it's used a lot, it's going to be tired. And if you're doing something that needs willpower, put it earlier in the day, and if that's not possible, maintain your willpower until you need it. Not easy to set up self-discipline instruction, though – several businesses have tried and failed. When you have poor self-discipline, the investigation is unlikely to attend or perform the research that is required.

A 1992 research in an orthopedic unit in Scotland found that patients would increase recovery levels after surgery if they prepare and predict how they can handle the pain involved in healing from joint operations. And if they're working on their own (not following someone else's strategy), and if the strategy is precise. No, not "if / when the pain comes, I will ..." but "when I get to the bus stop, my knee is going to hurt. If this happens, I'm going to sit on the seat for 5 minutes before I drive. Knowing their strategy also meant planning ahead and thinking about what to do when their urge to resist would be at its peak, hence the correlation with willpower.

Starbucks offers staff instructions to get used to tough situations, but the instruction manuals often include a lot of blank pages. That employee is expected to think ahead and find out what they're going to do when the cue occurs. And they populate their own instruction manual.

Muraven wondered why it was easy to create willpower in some cases and not in others. He noticed that when people were given a challenge that required determination, and they felt that they had a choice, or when they were asked in a pleasant way, it was simple. It needed less force of will. If people felt pressured or compelled to participate, more effort was required, and it was more difficult to promote. Therefore, giving workers a sense of autonomy will dramatically increase the amount of energy and concentration on their work. And vice versa; lack of control demands more effort, and it is possible that more errors will arise when / when they come to an end.

Howard Schultz, the man who transformed Starbucks into a colossus, is not so different from Travis in certain respects. He grew up on a public housing estate in Brooklyn, sharing a two-bedroom apartment with his parents and two siblings. While he was seven years old, Schultz 's father fractured his leg and lost his work of driving a diaper truck. This was what it took to put the family in crisis. His father, after he healed his ankle, started cycling through a series of low-paying jobs. "My dad never found his way," Schultz said to me. "I saw his self-esteem be broken. I thought there was so much more he should have done.

Schultz 's school was a wild, overcrowded place with asphalt playgrounds and children playing soccer, basketball, softball, punch ball, slap ball, and every other game they could think of. If your team has lost, it could take an hour to make another turn. So Schultz made sure that his team would always win, no matter what the cost. He would come home with raw scrapes on his elbows and knees that his mother would gently clean with a wet rag. "You 're not going to leave," she said.

His determination won him a college football scholarship (he fractured his jaw and never played a game), a degree in communications, and finally a career as a Xerox salesman in New York City. He would wake up every morning, go to a new midtown office building, take the elevator to the top floor, and go door-to-door, politely asking if anyone was interested in toners or copying machines. So he will take the elevator down one floor and start all over again.

Around the beginning of the 1980s, Schultz worked for a plastics company when he found that a little-known store in Seattle was buying a large number of coffee drip cones. Schultz flew out of here and fell in love with the service. Two years later, when he learned that Starbucks, then just six locations, was on sale, he begged everyone he knew for money and purchased it.

It was 1987. There were eighty-four stores in three years, more than a thousand in six years. There are seventeen thousand stores in more than fifty countries today.

Why did Schultz turn out to be so different from all the other children on the playground? Many of his former classmates are policemen and firemen in Brooklyn today. Others are in prison. Schultz 's worth more than $1 billion. He was named as one of the best CEOs of the twentieth century. How did he find the determination — the will — to switch from a housing project to a private jet?

"I don't know," he said. "My mom always said, 'You're going to be the first person to go to college, you're going to be a doctor, you're going to make us all proud.' She would ask these little questions, 'How are you going to prepare tonight? What are you going to do tomorrow, huh? How do you know if you're ready for the test? 'I was taught to set goals.

"I was really fortunate," he said. "And I really, sincerely believe that if you convince people that they have what it takes to succeed, they 're going to prove you right."

Schultz 's emphasis on employee preparation and customer service has made Starbucks one of the most profitable businesses in the world. For years, he had been directly interested in nearly every aspect of how the business was operated. Throughout 2000, drained, he turned over day-to-day activities to other executives, where Starbucks started to fail. Within a few years, consumers complained about the price of their drinks and customer service. Executives, focused on rapid expansion, have frequently dismissed complaints. Employees have been depressed. Surveys suggested that people were beginning to suit Starbucks with tepid coffee and fake smiles.

So Schultz stepped back to the position of Chief Executive Officer in 2008. Among his priorities was the overhaul of the company's training system with a view to renewing its emphasis on a range of topics, including bolstering employees—or "partners" in Starbucks' lingo—willpower and self-confidence. "We had to start winning customer and partner trust again," Schultz said.

Around the same time, a new wave of research emerged that looked at the study of motivation in a slightly different way. Researchers have found that certain individuals, such as Travis, have been able to build willpower patterns fairly easily. Others, however, failed, no matter how much preparation and support they had earned. Who makes the difference?

Mark Muraven, who was a professor at the University of Albany at the time, set up a new experiment. He placed the undergraduates in a room with a plate of soft, fresh cookies and told them to ignore the treats. Half of the participants were treated kindly. "We ask you not to eat cookies, please. Is that all right? "The researcher said that. Then she explained the purpose of the experiment, stating that it was to test their ability to resist temptations. She thanked them for their time. "If you have any ideas or thoughts about how we should enhance this project, please let me know. We want you to help us make the experience as good as possible.

The other half of the participants were not coddled the same way. They've just been given orders.

"You must not eat the cookies," the researcher said. She did not clarify the goals of the experiment, praise them, or display any interest in their suggestions. She ordered them to obey her instructions. "We 're going to start now," she said.

Students from both groups had to disregard the hot cookies for five minutes after the researcher left the room. None of them gave in to temptation.

Then the researcher came back. She asked every student to take a look at the computer monitor. It was coded to flash the numbers on the screen, one at a time, five hundred milliseconds apiece. Participants were asked to hit the space bar every time they saw a "6," followed by a "4." This has become a common way to test willpower — to pay attention to a repetitive series of blinking numbers takes a concentration comparable to working on an impossible puzzle.

Students who had been treated kindly did a decent job on the computer exam. Whenever the "6" blinked, and the "4" followed, they pounced onto the space bar. They've been able to keep their attention on the entire twelve minutes. We had the will to spare, despite missing cookies.

Students who had been treated rudely, on the other hand, had done awful things. They kept thinking about touching the space bar. We said they were tired and couldn't concentrate on it. Their willpower muscles, the researchers concluded, were sick of the unexpected orders.

As Muraven began to investigate why students who had been handled favorably had more determination, he found that the main difference was a sense of control over their experience. "We've seen that time and again," Muraven said to me. "If people are asked to do something that needs self-control if they believe they 're doing something for personal reasons — if they feel like it's a privilege or something they like because it benefits someone else — it's a lot less taxing. If they feel like they don't have control, if they just obey orders, their willpower muscles get exhausted much faster. In both cases, people have skipped cookies. Yet when students were treated like cogs, instead of men, it took a lot more willpower.

This perspective has important consequences for businesses and organizations. Just giving workers a sense of agency — a feeling like they are in charge, that they have a real decision-making authority — can significantly increase how much energy and attention they bring to their work. One 2010 research at a manufacturing plant in Ohio, for example, looked at assembly line employees who were encouraged to make minor choices about their schedules and work climate. They designed their own uniforms, and they had control over shifts. Anything much has changed. All production methods and pay rates remained the same. Productivity at the plant improved by 20% within two months. The staff took shorter breaks. They made fewer errors. Giving workers a sense of control increased how much self-discipline they carried to their jobs.

The same lessons are true for Starbucks. Today, the company focuses on giving workers a stronger sense of authority. They asked staff to rethink how espresso machines and cash registers are designed to determine for themselves how customers should be greeted and where the products should be displayed. It's not uncommon for a store manager to spend hours talking to his staff about where a blender should be stored.

"We started encouraging partners to use their intelligence and imagination, rather than telling them 'take the coffee out of the box, place the cup here, follow this law,'" said Kris Engskov, vice president of Starbucks. "People want to monitor their lives."

Turnover has already gone down. Customer service is over. Upon Schultz 's return, Starbucks has boosted sales by more than $1.2 billion a year.

While Travis was 16, his mother told him a story before he quit school and began working for Starbucks. They were driving together, and Travis asked why he had no more siblings. His mother had always wanted to be fully honest with her son, so she told him that she had been pregnant two years before Travis was born, but she had had had an abortion. They had two children at that point, she explained, and they were addicted to drugs. They didn't think they would be able to support another baby. And, one year later, she became pregnant with Travis. She was thinking about having another abortion, but it was too hard to handle. It was better to let nature follow its course. Travis was born there.

"She told me she had made a lot of mistakes, but it was one of the best things that ever happened to her to have me," Travis said. "If your parents are addicted, you grow up to know that you can't really trust them with everything you need. Yet I was lucky enough to meet the bosses who gave me what was missing. If my mom was as lucky as I was, I hope things would have turned out to be different for her.

A few years after that conversation, Travis's father called out to say that an infection had penetrated the bloodstream of his mother from one of the places on her arm she used to fire. Travis was then taken to the Lodi Hospital, but she was asleep when he arrived. She died half an hour later when she was taken out of life support.

A week later, Travis' father was in a pneumonia hospital. His lungs had collapsed. Travis drove back to Lodi, but it was 8:02 p.m. when he went to the emergency department. Then, a nurse told him he was going to have to come back tomorrow; the visit hours were over.

Since then, Travis has been thinking a lot about that moment. He hasn't begun working at Starbucks yet. He had not known how to control his feelings. He didn't have the patterns he 'd spent years cultivating since then. As he thinks about his life now, how far away he's from a world where accidents occur and stolen vehicles turn up in the driveways, and a nurse seems like an insurmountable barrier, he wonders how it's able to move such a long distance in such a short period of time.

"If he had died a year later, it would have been different," Travis told me. By then, he should have learned how to bargain with the nurse calmly. He must have learned to accept her jurisdiction, and then respectfully ask for a slight exemption. He may have been in the hospital. Because of that, he gave up and walked away. "I said, 'All I want to do is talk to him once,' and she said, 'He's not even awake, he's coming back tomorrow after visiting hours.' I didn't know what to say. I've felt so tiny.

The Father of Travis died that night.

Each year, on the anniversary of his death, Travis gets up early, takes an extra-long shower, prepares his daycare, and then drives to work. He's just arriving in time.

WHICH HABITS MATTER MOST

My top two qualities of effective people are "Developer" and "Achiever." That also shows you absolutely little about my potential to do anything or accomplish any unique outcomes.

I rated the lowest on the Kolbe as a Fast Start. It doesn't mean much, but over time, I've got to deal with real-life and work on the other ways I suck like Truth Finder, Follow Thru, and Implementor.

I choose the blue to the purple.

I feel more like a lion than a chimp.

I'm gritty, but I'm lazy too much. I resonate more with a circle than with a rectangle. Mostly, I eat a Mediterranean diet, but I like hamburgers. I enjoy hanging with people for a bit, but I still take a long time to disappear into isolation with a teapot and a thick journal. I shop for Whole Foods every week, but a lot of my lunchtime is spent in a cheap Mexican spot.

Nothing about all of this will tell you something, at all, about my skills, my chances of success, or my potential results.

So please, man, stop trying to bucket me into a "form" or presume that my "strongness" or experience gives me some advantage whatsoever. Labeling people hurts, no matter how it's done. I hear you say that these tests are meant to examine and know about myself, not to mark me or to guide me per se.

Yet wait, we know my perceived "strengths," and they somehow don't help my getaway. My normal instincts are not doing the job. As a dictator, I have to be honest — sometimes it's just not about who I am, what I want, or what I am naturally good at. It's about me rising to serve a mission, not a goal bowing down to match my limited power.

I know that you always want to talk about my history. You know I'm from the Midwest, but I live in California right now. My mom raised my sister and me on her own. She was a beauty stylist in the morning and a hostess at a restaurant in the evenings. Dad left us, and her when I was 14. I have decent qualifications. I've only been bullied once or twice. I liked playing golf at college. In about five years after college, I've been through two fairly terrible relationships. I've been shot already. Yet I have made some good friends, and I slowly gained confidence. I kind of fell through the job I'm doing right now, but it's awesome.

This history, too, does not tell you anything about my abilities. It doesn't offer any definite hints or direction to get ahead today.

Now, I'm just honest with you. I know that you like personality tests and ask me about my history. But if someone has a history and a story, then obviously the history of the tale of an individual is not what gives them an advantage.

I guess I'm showing you I can do the navel-gazing just fine on my own. I asked you to convince me what you needed to do to get to the next point.

I need to know what to do with it. What habits do you have, regardless of personality?

Don't tell me who the top performers are. Ask me what they're doing at the granular stage, through programs that can be repeated. This level of clarity is the diamond.

Find that for me, and you've got a customer for life.

Otherwise, it's time to divide the forms.

Late in my career, I got this e-mail from Tom, a coaching partner. This caught me by surprise, to say the least. Tom was a kind guy, a good leader. He was creative and still ready to do new things.1 An e-mail like that, putting our working partnership on alert until I considered "lime," was rare for him. The follow-up talk I had with him was even more transparent. He was somewhat exasperated.

Tom was searching for results. Even back then, I wasn't sure how to get them.

It was nearly ten years ago. Back then, when I was just a "life coach" run-of-the-mill, it was popular to do four things and find out how to help someone boost their results.

This also began asking the client questions about what he or she wanted, and what "limiting values" got in the way. You also asked them about the past, attempting to find certain incidents that could affect present habits.

Second, you've used evaluation methods better to evaluate personality traits, habits, and interests. The aim was to help people better understand themselves and any actions that could allow them to succeed. Popular methods included Myers-Briggs, Clifton StrengthsFinder, Kolbe ATM Database, and

DiSC Analysis. Life coaches will also employ qualified professionals or consultants to help handle these resources.

Second, the mentor will be sifting through experience by feedback evaluations and talking to others around the company, using 360-degree surveys to find out how others viewed them and what they expected through them. You 'd speak about the people around whom they lived and worked.

Third, you should determine their real performance. You 'd look at their previous outcomes and see what stuck out, what methods allowed them to do a successful performance, how much they wanted to make a difference.

And I did all these things in this tradition. Since Tom liked concrete statistics and analyses, we spent a lot of time analyzing the tests. We collaborated with a variety of high-level contractors who were specialists in different methods. We've got binders full of information.

Instead, over the course of two years, despite understanding my client's characteristics, strengths, ratings, and history, I kept watching him struggle.

I felt bad. I couldn't find out why he didn't get the answers he needed. This was around the time he received an e-mail.

Quick forward to ten years since Tom's e-mail, and now I'm fortunate to have one of the world's biggest personal and career learning labs — which is how we conceive about my worldwide community and platforms — in the nation. The following includes more than eleven million followers through my Twitter pages; two million more subscribers to the newsletter; one and a half million students who have attended my video series or educational courses; thousands of participants at our multi-day live high-performance seminars; millions of writers of books and articles on inspiration, spirituality, and life-changing topics; and more than half of my readership. This community has driven my personal video creation to surpass 100,000 web views — all without a single cat video.

Something is interesting about the group is that they come to us specifically for personal growth guidance and instruction, which gives us an enlightening perspective of what people are dealing with, what they think they desire in life, and what makes them improve. At the High-Performance Center, we use this large audience to take polls, administer interviews, mine student behavior, and opinion info, and research before and after outcomes from online training courses and one-to-one success coaching sessions. Any time we try to learn more about human nature and high efficiency, we 're going to our lab for insights.

Many of what we have observed from these large markets and data sets sounds like common sense. To be good, hard work, dedication, discipline, endurance, and people's skills are always more important than IQ, natural talent, or where you're from. Nothing here will come as a shock, as this information correlates with current work on achievement and world-class results. Read some of the new social sciences (and I've offered a couple of advice if you choose to research the studies for yourself), and you'll find that progress in general, in virtually any attempt, is made possible by malleable factors — things you can alter and strengthen through attempt. For instance:

- ✓ Pick up the thought that you want to follow.

- ✓ Add the attention you offer to your interests and the intensity with which you seek them.

- ✓ Pick up the amount of work you devote yourself to.

- ✓ Look up the way you think and handle others.

✓ Enter the diligence and constancy with which you aspire to accomplish your goals.

✓ Take up the way you come back from your defeats.

The amount of regular activity you do to keep your brain and body healthy and take care of your general well-being [citations]

What has arisen in our research and in science and scholarly studies is that achievement is accomplished not by a particular category of individual, but rather by individuals from all walks of life who follow a similar collection of activities. The query that inspired this book was, "What, exactly, are the most effective practices?

FINDING WHAT MATTERS

For the past few years, we've been zeroing on what pushes the needle forward to help people reach long-term results. And we discovered what Tom understood intuitively: successful performers do things differently than others, and their behaviors can be repeated through tasks (and almost any situation) regardless of the temperament, history, or interests. In fact, we've found that there are six intentional patterns that have made much of the difference in success results across domains. Even your strongest talents or innate ability are moot without the practices of promoting them.

We used applicable ideas from scientific research, evidence from our regional study, and feedback from over three thousand high-performance coaching sessions to discover the most critical patterns. We then pooled all these inputs to create organized interview questions that could be posed by high-performing performers.

PROCESS

We identified high-performing participants by common social science methods, such as sample recognition and quantitative success metrics (e.g., academic achievement, athletic results, measurable business, and financial outcomes, etc.). For example, we asked people how strongly they agreed with statements like the following:

✓ Most of my colleagues would think of me as a high performer.

✓ In the past three years, I have usually achieved a high degree of success.

✓ If "high performance" is described as excellence with what you do over the long term, relative to other people, I'm known as a high performer.

✓ In my main area of specialization, I have had more influence than any of my colleagues for a longer time.

For those who clearly agreed with these claims, we then administered one-on-one interviews with them (and also with their peers). We also took supplementary surveys to ask high-performing self-reported questions, such as:

✓ Once you launch a new project, what do you do, deliberately and systematically, to set yourself up to win?

✓ Which personal and professional habits are there to help you remain focused, energized, imaginative, efficient, and effective? (In effect, we asked for every trait.)

✓ What habits have you begun and abandoned, and what habits have you kept that still seem to work?

✓ What recurrent thoughts or assumptions will you intentionally say to yourself, to do your best as you (a) go through new circumstances, (b) react to adversity or frustration, and (c) support others?

✓ If you were to distinguish the three aspects that made you successful, and you realized that you could employ just the three in the next big project again, what would these three things be?

✓ If you're practicing for a meeting (or match, results, scenario, conversation) that really matters, how are you going about (a) your planning and (b) your practice?

✓ If you take on a big new team initiative tomorrow, what, precisely, would you say and do to make your team successful?

- ✓ What activities earn you fast results, and which are longer-term behaviors that make you stand out?

- ✓ How do you preserve or secure your well-being while you are under threat from a near-term deadline?

- ✓ How do you normally do to yourself as you express self-doubt or frustration or fear like you are failing?

- ✓ Which makes you comfortable, and how can you "turn on" confidence when you need it?

- ✓ Why do you handle coping with other people in your life who (a) support you, (b) do not help you, and (c) want to help you, but who do not?

- ✓ What habits are keeping you happy and safe while you aspire for greater goals?

Such questions, and hundreds more like them, helped us begin to narrow down the factors and behaviors that high performers have identified as causing the greatest difference in their performance. Clear themes emerged, and an initial list of nearly two dozen high-performance patterns was drawn up.

Next, we carried out surveys to the general public, including questions close to those posed by self-reported high-performers. After researching the behaviors better distinguished high performers from those in our general surveys, we narrowed the list even further. At the end of the day, we walled it down to the patterns that were intentional, measurable, malleable, workable, and, most importantly, efficient across realms. That is, we needed behaviors that would allow someone to be effective not just in one area of expertise, but across a wide range of topics, events, and industries. We required patterns that anyone, everywhere, in any sphere of activity, could apply over and over again to a tangible improvement in performance.

After we established HP6, we worked to perform further literature reviews and confirmation checks. We also developed an empirical variant of the High-Performance Indicator (HPI) based on six behaviors as well as other proven success indicators. We tested the HPI pilot with more than 30,000 people from 195 countries, and quantitatively confirmed its validity, reliability, and usefulness.

HP6 will help you succeed whether you are a college, an artist, a president, a CEO, an athlete, or a home parent. Whether you're good or not, these habits will help you reach the next level.

While hundreds of other variables that affect your long-term success — luck, timing, social support, or unexpected artistic breakthroughs, to name a few — the HP6 is under your influence and boosts your results more than anything else we've measured.

If you want to reach higher levels of performance with anything you do, you will always do the following:

✓ Seek clarity about who you want to be, how you want to communicate with others, what you want, and what gives you the greatest meaning. As every mission or new effort starts, you ask questions like, "What kind of person do I want to be while I'm doing this? "How can I handle others? "What are my goals and objectives? "How will I concentrate on that will offer me a sense of purpose and fulfillment? "Such kinds of questions are posed by top performers not only at the outset of the project but frequently throughout. They do not just "get clarity" once and create a mission statement that stands the test of time; they constantly seek clarity again and again as times change and as they take on new projects or on new social situations. This kind of daily self-monitoring is one of the hallmarks of progress.

✓ Produce energy so that you can retain concentration, commitment, and well-being. You'll need to take active control of your mental stamina, physical energy, and positive emotions in very clear ways to stay in your A-game.

✓ You were raising the need for outstanding results. This involves consciously digging into the motivations why you simply will do well. The desire is focused on a combination of the internal requirements (e.g., personality, convictions, ideals, or aspirations of excellence) and external pressures (e.g., moral responsibilities, competitiveness, public duties, deadlines). It's about just understanding why and stoking the fire all the time, so you have the push or energy you need to get on it.

✓ Increase profitability In your main field of concern. In specific, concentrate on prolific production performance (PQO) in the region where you want to be recognized and drive effects. You'll also need to eliminate obstacles (including opportunities) that rob your focus from building PQO.

✓ Create Power With those around you. It would make you happier to get people to trust in and support your goals and aspirations. Unless you actively develop a positive support network, major achievements over the long term are all but unlikely.

✓ Show courage By voicing your thoughts, behaving confidently, and standing up for yourself and others, even in the face of fear, confusion, danger, or changing circumstances. Courage is not an accidental act, and it is a function of preference and will.

Look for an explanation. Generate your electricity. Raise the need. Growing your profitability. Build your power. Demonstrate your bravery. Here are the six habits you need to follow if you want to achieve high efficiency in any situation. In the hundreds of personal actions and social activities we've studied, these practices push the needle the most to significantly improve results.

You may have noticed that nowhere in this list is it said to reflect on your inherent gifts, abilities, strengths, history, or power. That's because no matter how fantastic a personality you have, how many supposed natural qualities you have, how much wealth you have, how talented you are, how creative you are, what talents you have acquired, or how well you have achieved in the past — none of these things would mean a lot on your own. It wouldn't care if you didn't know what you needed and how to achieve it (clarity), felt too worn out to succeed (energy), didn't have a sense of motivation or an incentive to get things done (necessity), couldn't concentrate and produce results that matter the most (productivity), didn't have people's skills to get others to believe in you or help you (influence), or didn't speak up for yourself, because it didn't. Without HP6, even the most talented person will be lost, exhausted, unmotivated, unproductive, lonely, or afraid.

Effectiveness in life is not the product of relying on what is automatic, simple, or normal for us. Rather, it is the product of how we actively aspire to face the tougher challenges of life, evolve beyond our comforts, and actively seek to transcend our prejudices and expectations, so that we can learn, respect, serve, and lead others.

As I make this point, people sometimes scoff at the success of the "strengths" campaign. Personally, I am a fan of any resources that help people know more about themselves. I do deeply respect Gallup, the company that led the strength-based movement. Yet I do not suggest that people use the presumption of power to lead others or to reach the next level of achievement in their own lives. The movement of strengths is based on the belief that we have "innate" strengths — the gifts for which we are born. This means that we are "naturally" good at certain things from birth and that we may as well be concentrating on those things. Without a doubt, that's a feel-good recipe, and it's definitely better than being obsessed with our shortcomings all the time.

My only question about the movement of strengths is that, in a dynamic and constantly changing environment, reaching the top does not necessarily come to everyone. Irrespective of what you are inherently good at, to get better, you must go beyond what came inherently to you at birth or in your teen years, right? That's why the inherent claim doesn't hold so well. In order to achieve exceptional success and succeed over the long term, you will need to evolve far beyond what is simple or normal to you, because the real world is full of complexity and ever-increasing demands for development. Your "natural" birth abilities are not going to be enough. As Tom said in his e-mail to me at the beginning of this chapter,

If you have great aspirations to do incredible things, you will have to evolve and expand far beyond what is normal to you. To rise to high success, you're going to have to focus on weaknesses, build completely new skill sets beyond what you consider easy or what you want to do. It's supposed to be common sense: if you really want to make a mark, you're going to have to evolve more to offer more, and it won't feel easy or normal.

In the end, even if you don't agree with my thought process here, understanding your personality style or perceived inherent abilities isn't all that helpful at helping you reach the next big target in unpredictable environments.

To my friends and colleagues running companies: let's avoid wasting all this money on costly strengths and personality tests in futile attempts to categorize people, and instead concentrate on educating our employees invalidated behaviors that everyone can use to enhance their performance.

The good news is that no one "innately" lacks any high-performance behaviors. Strong performers are not lucky stiffs fitted with a large bag of strengths at birth. We actually apply the behaviors we've addressed, and they do so more frequently than their peers. This is it. That is the difference.

And it doesn't matter if you're an extrovert or an independent thinker, an INTJ or an ESFP, a Christian or an atheist, a Spaniard or a Singaporean, an artist or an engineer, a manager or a CEO, a successor or an analyst, a mom or a Martian — the six high-performance behaviors each have the ability to have a significant effect on the places that matter most to you. Together, they have the ability to revolutionize your success in every important area of your life.

You're not meant to be innately fantastic at HP6. You've got to work at them all the time. Whenever you're hoping to succeed with a new target, mission, or vision, you've got to shut down the HP6. Each time you find yourself operating below your full potential, put your HP6 to bear. When you ever wonder why you're struggling in something, just take the HPI and find out which behaviors you 're scoring low in. Then make the area better, and you'll be back on track.

This intentional emphasis is an important distinction, particularly as it frees us from the idea that success comes more "naturally" to some than to others. Looking through my decade to represent so many elite-level achievers as well as all our surveys and professional evaluations, we just haven't seen high performance consistently correlate strongly with personality, Intelligence, innate talent, imagination, years of experience, gender, race, culture, or compensation.

In the last two decades of neuroscience and positive psychology research, researchers have begun to notice the same thing and to transform the old model on its head. How we do for what we have appears to be far more critical than what we have in the first place. What you are innately good at is less important than how you choose to see the world, to establish yourself, to lead others, and to remain persistent despite the difficulty.

A lot of employees are high paying, but not high-performing. Anyone in a company that has had their staff evaluate their strengths will certainly testify that many of their colleagues know their strengths, and also work on their strengths, but still struggle to do a better job. And like every great company culture, there are often high performers and low performers. Why? Why? Since high performance is not a particular type of person. It's not about winning the genetic lottery, how long you've served, the color of your eyes, how many people are helping you, or what you're paying for. It's about your success habits — which you have full control of.

This point is worth hammering home since so many people are using these explanations to justify their bad results. Only imagine how much you say things like:

- ✓ "I just don't have the charisma to get ahead of me. I'm just not [extrovert, intuitive, charismatic, accessible, conscientious].

- ✓ "I'm just not the smartest person in the house."

- ✓ "I'm just not, of course, gifted like they are. Ah, I wasn't born good at that. I don't have the right balance of energy.

- ✓ References to "I'm not a right-minded guy."

- ✓ "I don't have enough experience."

- ✓ "I'm a [woman, black male, a Hispanic, middle-aged white man, immigrant], and that's why I'm not going to succeed."

- ✓ "My business culture doesn't help me."

- ✓ "I would have been a lot happier if they paid me what I'm actually worth."

It's time for all of us to recognize these reasons for what they are: lame excuses for under-optimal results, particularly over the long term.

It's not to say that the underlying variables don't matter at all. There is good evidence that they are significant, particularly in childhood growth, and many of these factors can have a dramatic effect on your mood, actions, decisions, health, and relationship as an adult.

Leaders should take note: relying on all of the factors I listed in that list does not get you far enough to help your people boost their performance. Such variables are just not that straightforward to describe, handle, or improve.

Suppose, for example, that you're working on a project with a couple of teammates. In particular, you have one person that doesn't work well.

Imagine how ridiculous it would be for you to go over and say:

- ✓ If you could only make your personality easier for us.

- ✓ If you could only get your IQ up for us.

- ✓ If you could only alter the way, you were innately born.

- ✓ If you could only be a bit more right-brained.

- ✓ If you could have just five more years of experience under your belt here.

- ✓ If you could only be more [Asian, black, white, male, female].

- ✓ If you could just improve the culture here, it's very easy.

- ✓ If you could only give yourself the right amount to be more successful.

You 're getting the idea. These are clearly not appropriate categories to be addressed.

The bottom line is that if you're going to focus on anything to boost your success or your team's performance, continue with the HP6.

RISING TIDE LIFTS ALL BOATS — ONE HABIT LIFTS ALL OTHER

We like to think of the HP6 as "meta-habits" as they make all the other good habits in life fall into place. By finding clarification, you develop a habit of asking questions, looking inward, analyzing your actions, evaluating whether you're on track. By generating energy, you'll be better off, eat healthier, exercise more. And so on, man.

What is interesting about our HP6 work is that each change in one field enhances the other. This means that if you increase clarity, you 're likely to see energy change, need, efficiency, bravery, and power. Our analysis also suggests that although people with high ratings appear to be high on one habit the other, each habit gives them a little extra edge by increasing the overall high-performance score. Develop just one of these behaviors and boost your performance.

Another interesting thing we've learned is that all HP6 predicts overall happiness, which means the higher the score in any habit, the greater the chances you'll report being happy in life. Taken together, though, the HP6 is a strong indicator not only of whether you're a good performer but also of whether you're satisfied.

Is there a state of mind of high performance?

People also ask me if there is a particular "condition" that will make it possible for them to succeed in the long term. Okay, by nature, emotional and mental states don't last. They 're brief, man. Moods hang around longer, and patterns remain the longest, which is why we're concentrating on them.

Yet I think what people really want is, "How do I feel when I hit high performance? What do you think it feels like, so I can reverse engineer that? The data will answer the query.

In a keyword review of the data from the public survey of more than thirty thousand high-performing respondents, it is very clear: when people speak about how high-performance people feel, they report feeling complete dedication, happiness, and trust (in that order). This means that they appear to be completely involved in what they're doing, appreciate what they're doing, and trust their ability to work things out.

Rounding out the top five was purposefulness and flow, as in "I feel like I'm in the flow." ("In the zone" was not a choice in our surveys as it was a phrase rather than a word, but the most popular written-in descriptor.) Determination, concentration, aim, purposefulness, and conscientiousness rounded out the top terms that people used to explain what they felt to be in high performance.

Knowing this, you may as well start thinking towards the end.

Start paying your full attention to the moments of your life. Continue bringing more happiness to you. Start to put more confidence. Those aspects will not only make you feel better, but they will also help you work better. Also, the same caveat applies to states as to strengths: without good behaviors, it's just not enough.

THE HP6

The HP6 offered me a validated game plan to excel in my life ventures. We are now a normal operating system for joining every new situation. I used them throughout my professional life, and the findings were impressive and very public.

Beyond myself, the practices and ideas in this book have profoundly changed the lives of hundreds of thousands of our students. These students take the HPI before and after our online classes, live training activities, and coaching experience. They enjoy seeing the demonstrable evidence that they're changing their lives. Our students are continually increasing their overall high achievement (and overall life satisfaction) ranking significantly. We have used the HPI in organizations to help them define where their employees and teams will focus their growth.

In addition, we have seen positive outcomes through client coaching strategies. Over ten thousand hour coaching sessions conducted by accredited Certified High-Performance CoachesTM prove that people can significantly improve their actions and achieve higher success in many aspects of their lives in weeks, not years.

It is not to say that high-performance practices are a magic bullet for all life's problems. For the last decade, as a high-performance coach and researcher, I've been searching for a lot of disabling evidence for HP6, so I'm glad to share it with you.

In finding unconfirmed facts, we've been searching for people who are not high performing while following the behaviors in this book. Are there people in the world who actively pursue clarification, generate strength, increase need, increase efficiency, build power, and display bravery who are, in reality, underperformers or even failures? I've never found this to be the case, but common sense suggests there's bound to be an exception. Can anyone neglect one of these habits and still be successful? For example, can someone be a crazy success but still lack clarity? It's in total. Can anyone have no bravery and yet be a success? You bet that they will.

Yet note, here we're not thinking about the initial success. It is the long term we 're talking about.

Odds are, if you miss any of the HP6 for too long, your high success scores (and happiness ratings) will decrease. You just wouldn't be as successful or as exceptional as you should have been.

Many critics would argue that our explanations of high-performance behaviors or phrases used in the HPI are too ambiguous or open to interpretation. Of course, this is often a possibility when explaining human actions. If we claim that someone "has grit," "is imaginative," "is an extrovert," or "is struggling to keep concentration," we may also argue that those statements are ambiguous or generic. But that doesn't mean that we're not going to seek to describe, calculate, or teach people about them. Studying human psychology is an imprecise attempt, but it's worth a job because it lets us understand what makes us work well. All we can do is use the validated but unreliable resources available and continue to do so on how to explain and compare the claims and patterns that are relevant for high performers. That's just what we've been doing.

In addition to constantly trying to disprove our own hypotheses, we have tried to address self-reporting prejudices by testing to see that what respondents reported in our initial surveys was accurate in their real lives. We achieved so by interviewing them randomly, contrasting objective performance metrics, and receiving peer input.

Much of the time, we've found that people share their truthful answers in this sector, as they want to determine precisely where they are and figure out where they can develop.

We have used reverse statements and scores in many of our surveys to see if the answers were accurate.

Like any researcher, I'm always open to new facts, and I look at the results, including those in this book, as just another messy phase in the long march of understanding people and how they function. I'll remind you, and I'm not a psychologist, psychiatrist, neuroscientist, biologist, or any other word I 'm aware of that ends up in "-ist." I'm a qualified high-performance coach and trainer who pays for outcomes, not debate or theory. So that, ultimately, predisposes me to what I saw at college. And while I feel fortunate that I have been the most paid and most followed in the world on this subject, I am without doubt as flawless as any writer or professional attempting to deal with a subject of such magnitude and complexity. I've got a lot more to know about high results. There's a lot that this whole area doesn't know yet, and it needs to be discussed. What are the consequences of mental illness, childhood experiences, and socio-economic and neurobiological influences on the development and maintenance of these habits? Which of the activities has the needle most shifted to different sectors, professions, or educational levels?

In this book, I freely encourage you to ask your own questions as well as to challenge my assertions. In our published posts, I freely called for more testing of our proposals, and I'd love to hear your suggestions, too. Every day, my team and I try to learn more and more about this topic. I'm going to research it for good. I would love to know what works for you and what doesn't work for you. And whether or not you agree with what you're going to find in the pages below, I'm just recommending that you keep what works for you and delete the rest.

Test It for Yourself

Can the HP6 deliver as dramatic results for you as we've seen in our testing, training, and coaching? I 'd love to check it with you. That's why, once again, I 'm asking you to decide how successful these habits are. In case you haven't been around to follow my advice in the previous chapter until you read any more, take the HPI. It just takes a few minutes, and it's free online at HighPerformanceIndicator.com. It's going to give you a score on each of the six habits, and no, it's not going to mark you. Please take the survey. Do it right now. And be sure to enter your e-mail so that I can give you another connection to take the assessment again in seven to ten weeks. (Between now and then, read this book and watch the videos that you will receive after you take the assessment so that you have the tools you need to improve.) After a couple of weeks, you'll know from your own reaction to the assessment how much this work will help to change your life.

One thing is abundantly clear from our findings: you can never wait to fulfill a vision or add value out of fear that you may lack the "right things."

Where I grew up, we had this saying, "The time to have a map is before you reach the jungle." Maybe someday, you'll find yourself in an unpredictable position where your success really matters. Until that day, read this book and begin the six high-performance habits. This is your map, and it's going to take you through the thicket of life to the highest level of success.

SECRETS TO DEVELOP HABITS THAT MATTER

The end of the year is a wonderful time to stop, look back, and see how far you've come. Give yourself a pat on the back, because much of your success is due to the behaviors and rituals you've put in place.

While cultivating these habits may be crucial to the success of an entrepreneur, adhering to them requires practice and discipline.

Try pushing your patterns to the next stage with your New Year's resolution. Below are three guidelines for this:

1. Speak about the final product. I see people wasting so much time, effort, and not on the actual activity they 're trying to

introduce to their routine. They make a list, fill up their schedule, and even find someone to act as a supportive friend — all in the name of the habit. Avoid wasting your time formulating a pattern instead of concentrating on the result. My advice is to spend some time visualizing what kind of habit you 're going to make. Which is the product of this new habit?

2. Have an aim in your mind. You have years — or maybe decades — of experience under your belt. The way you did things, the habits you put in place, you got right here right now. When you're going to adjust, you 're going to have to do something differently.

So if you want to break a lifelong habit or make a new one, you have to have a common target that you're working towards, and it should be tangible—the more precise, the better. There must be something you 're working on that you can break down to a quantification point. For example, if you want to be more punctual, consider writing down how long every job actually takes. It will help you to observe where you may be wasting time (i.e., checking emails), which may cause you to be constantly delayed.

3. Many days, less time now. If you pick up a new habit, it means that it's not easy by nature. That's why it's not a habit. Once you get going, go easy on yourself. Consider it all right to do less of a routine, but more often for a particular time span, like a week or a month.

When I wanted to make it a routine to get in shape, I chose to become a triathlete. I can't start counting the number of seven-minute workouts in the first year. Indeed, I've just worked out for a really short time. My reasoning was, "I 'd rather do it five days a week, for as much time as I have, than hang on to some idea that a workout isn't a workout unless it's a certain period of time." And it worked.

HOW LEADERS CREATE HABITS THROUGH ACCIDENT AND DESIGN

No institutional habits, there are no organizations. There are only instances where they are deliberately built, and instances where they are made without forethought. Both businesses have unheard-of processes that make it possible to operate; otherwise, company members will never be able to keep up with all the different permutations of decision-making that front-line employees contend with every day. When a company may think that it makes deliberate decisions by structured research and development processes, thousands of converging patterns, procedures, and behaviors are ultimately responsible.

If you were asked by some new colleagues how to succeed in your business, it is doubtful that you will refer them to the policy manual. You should teach them instead of informal laws, truces between company departments, and lines that should not be crossed. When you work in a productive organization, that is possible because the company's members have developed organizational practices that provide a balance of influence and preserve stability, but also make it clear who is in charge.

By the early 2000s, Rhode Island Hospital was considered one of the nation's leading medical institutions. Nevertheless, the toxic atmosphere created by greedy doctors who mistreated nurses and ignored their advice contributed to a series of tragic mistakes, fines, and negative publicity in the operating rooms. The hospital became a poster child for medical mistakes, criticized by local and national media. This was a true disaster, and the new Chief Quality Officer used the situation as an incentive to introduce improvements that had already been introduced but were blocked.

Video cameras were mounted in the operating rooms, checklists were provided for each operation, and an anonymous reporting system was placed in place. Such improvements, in addition to modern training programs that underscored stronger coordination, allowed nurses to prevent operating errors. As a result, the hospital has since received many prestigious awards for the quality of its care.

The patient was unconscious while he was in the operating room at Rhode Island Hospital. His mouth was tense, his eyes closed, and the top of the tube of intubation peered over his lips. When a nurse hooked him up to a pump that would push oxygen into his lungs during surgery, one of his arms fell off the gurney, his face dotted in liver spots.

The guy was 86 years old, and he had collapsed at home three days ago. Afterward, he had trouble sitting up and answering questions, so then, his wife called the ambulance. In the emergency room, the doctor told him what had happened, but the man kept nodding in the middle of his sentence. The scan of his head showed why: the fall smashed his brain into his skull, triggering what is known as a subdural hematoma. Blood was pooling in the left portion of his cranium, pressing into the fragile layers of tissue inside his skull. The fluid had been building up for almost seventy-two hours, and the parts of the brain that regulated his breathing and his heart had started to fade. The man would die unless the blood were drained.

At the time, Rhode Island Hospital was one of the nation's leading medical institutions, the largest teaching hospital for Brown University, and the only trauma center in southeastern New England. Inside the tall brick and glasshouse, doctors have pioneered state-of-the-art medical methods, including the use of ultrasound waves to kill tumors within the patient's body. In 2002, the National Coalition for Health Care ranked the hospital's intensive care unit as one of the best in the world.

Yet when the elderly patient arrived, Rhode Island Hospital already had another reputation: a location riven by internal tensions. There were intense, simmering enmities between nurses and doctors. In 2000, the Nursing Union voted to strike after arguing that they had been forced to work excessively long hours. More than three hundred of them were standing outside the hospital with signs reading "Stop Slavery" and "They can't take away our pride."

"This place can be horrible," a nurse said to a reporter. "The doctors will make you feel like you are useless like you are disposable. Like you need to be grateful to clean up after them.

By the end of the day, administrators decided to limit nurses' mandatory overtime, but tensions continued to increase. A few years later, a surgeon was preparing for routine abdominal surgery when a nurse called for a "time-out." These delays are common practice in most hospitals, a way for physicians and nurses to ensure that errors are prevented. The nurses at Rhode Island Hospital were insistent on time-outs, particularly after the surgeon mistakenly removed the tonsils of a girl who was supposed to have had eye surgery. Time-outs were intended to catch up with these mistakes before they occurred.

After the abdominal surgery, when the OR nurse told the team to assemble around the patient for a time-out to discuss their strategy, the doctor went to the door.

"Why aren't you leading this? "The surgeon asked the nurse about it. "I'm going to make a call outside. Knock when you're ready to go.

"You 're going to be here for this, Nurse," she said.

"You can do it," said the surgeon as he moved toward the door.

"Professor, I don't think that's accurate."

The doctor avoided looking at her. "If I want your damn opinion, I'm going to ask for it," he said. "Never again doubt my authority. If you can't do your job, get the hell out of my OR.

The nurse-led the time-out collected the doctor a few minutes later, and the operation was uncomplicated. She never questioned the physician again, and never said anything when such protection protocols were violated.

"Some doctors were great, and others were monsters," said one nurse who worked at Rhode Island Hospital in the mid-2000s. "We called it a glass factory, and it seemed like it might collapse at any minute."

In order to cope with these tensions, the staff formed informal rules — habits peculiar to the institution — which helped to avert the most apparent conflicts. Nurses, for example, often double-checked the instructions of error-prone doctors and secretly made sure the accurate doses were taken; they took extra time to write clearly on the patient records so that the hasty surgeon would not make the incorrect cut. One nurse told me that they were creating a system of color codes to alert each other. "We put the names of the doctors in various colors on the whiteboards," she said. "Blue meant 'sweet,' red meant 'jerk,' and black meant, 'whatever you do, don't contradict them, or they're going to tear your head off.'"

The Rhode Island Hospital was a place full of corrosive society. In comparison to Alcoa, where the deliberately crafted keystone habits around workplace health had contributed to greater and greater results, in Rhode Island Hospital, flying habits emerged among nurses trying to compensate for medical ignorance. The procedures of the hospital were not properly thought out. Rather, they arose by mistake, spreading by whispered warnings, before toxic trends emerged. It can happen within any company where the patterns are not deliberately planned. Just as choosing the right keystone patterns can bring about enormous change, the wrong ones can cause disasters.

And when the practices of the Rhode Island Hospital imploded, they made awful errors.

When the emergency room workers saw the brain scans of an 86-year - older man with a subdural hematoma, the neurosurgeon was instantly on duty. He was in the midst of routine spinal surgery, but when he got the message, he jumped out of the operating table and stared at the pictures of the older man's head on the computer screen. The surgeon told his assistant — a nurse practitioner — to go to the emergency room to get the man's wife to sign a consent form to authorize the operation. He ended the spinal operation. Half an hour later, the older man was taken to the same operating theatre.

Nurses have been running about. The unconscious older man had been put on the table. The nurse picked up his consent form and his medical chart.

"Dr," said the nurse, pointing at the patient chart. "The consent form does not say where the hematoma is." The nurse leafed through the paperwork. There was no clear sign on which side of his head they were expected to work.

Each hospital relies on paperwork to direct surgery. Until any cuts are made, a patient or family member must sign a document approving each procedure and checking the specifics. In a stressful atmosphere where as many as a dozen physicians and nurses will treat a patient between the ER and the recovery room, consent forms provide reminders to keep track of what is going to happen. No one will go to surgery without a signed and thorough consent.

"I've seen the scans before," said the surgeon. "It was on the right side of the brain. If we don't do this soon, he's going to die.

"Maybe we should bring the movies up again," said the nurse, turning toward the computer terminal. For security purposes, after 15 minutes of idling, the hospital's machines were closed. It will take at least a minute for the nurse to log in and upload the patient's brain scans to the computer.

"We don't have time," said the surgeon. "They told me he was going to crash. We need to ease the burden.

"What happens if we find the family? "The nurse asked.

"If that's what you want, call the fucking ER and find the boys! In the meantime, I 'm going to save his life. "The surgeon picked up the papers, scribbled" yes "on the consent document, and initialed it.

"Here," he said. "We've got to work immediately. The nurse had been operating at Rhode Island Hospital for a year.

He knew the atmosphere of the hospital. The name of this physician, the nurse, learned, was always scribbled in black on a broad whiteboard in the corridor, suggesting that nurses should be vigilant. In this case, the unwritten rules were clear: the surgeon always wins. The nurse put down the chart and stood aside as the doctor placed the older man's head in a cradle that provided access to the right side of his skull and shaved and applied an antiseptic to his scalp.

The intention was to open the skull and suction the blood on the top of his head. The surgeon cut off a flap of skin, uncovered the skull, and placed a hammer on the white bone. He started pressing before the bit broke through with a gentle pop. He had made two more holes and used a saw to carve out a triangular section of the man's skull. Below was the dura, the transparent sheath around the spine. "Oh my God," said someone.

There was no hematoma in it.

We were working on the wrong side of the brain. "We need him to be switched!

"The surgeon screamed.

The bone triangle was removed and reassembled with small metal plates, and screws and the patient's scalp was sewed. His head was relocated to the other side and then, again, shaved, cleansed, cut, and drilled before the skull triangle could be removed. This time, the hematoma was clearly apparent, a dark bulge poured like a thick liquid when the dura was pierced. The surgeon vacuumed the blood, and instantly the pressure inside the older man's skull dropped. The surgery, which was expected to take about an hour, took almost twice as long.

Afterward, the patient was taken to the intensive care unit, but he never regained full consciousness. He died two weeks later.

Subsequent reports suggested that it was difficult to ascertain the precise cause of death, but the patient's family argued that the pain of the surgical mistake had overwhelmed his already frail body, that the tension of extracting two pieces of the skull, the extra time of surgery, and the delay in evacuating the hematoma had pushed him over the edge. If it weren't for the error, they said, he would still be alive. The hospital paid for a settlement, and the surgeon was barred from operating at Rhode Island Hospital again.

Such an accident, some nurses believed later, was inevitable. The bureaucratic practices of the Rhode Island Hospital were so unhealthy, and it was only a matter of time before a major mistake occurred. 1 Of course, it's not just hospitals that breed dangerous habits. Destructive organizational practices can be observed in hundreds of sectors and thousands of companies. And almost always, they are the results of thoughtlessness, of leaders who ignore thinking about culture and thus allow it to evolve without guidance. No institutional practices, there are no organizations. There are only places where they are purposefully built, and places where they are created without forethought so that they sometimes develop out of competition or fear.

Yet often, even harmful patterns can be changed by leaders who know how to find the right opportunity. Sometimes, the right patterns arise in the midst of a crisis.

Once An Evolutionary Theory of Economic Change was first published in 1982, very few people outside of academics knew it. The book's bland cover and intimidating first sentence—"In this volume, we are establishing an evolutionary theory of the capacities and actions of business companies operating in a market setting, and building and evaluating a variety of models consistent with that theory"—almost seemed intended to discourage readers. The authors, Yale professors Richard Nelson and Sidney Winter, were best known for a series of highly theoretical articles discussing Schumpeterian theory that only the majority of Ph.D. candidates did not claim to understand.

Within the world of corporate management and organizational theory, however, the book went off like a rocket. Then it was hailed as one of the most important texts of the century. Economics professors started talking about it to business school colleagues, who began talking to CEOs at conferences, and soon executives cited Nelson and Winter inside companies as different from General Electric, Pfizer, and Starwood Hotels.

Nelson and Winter spent more than a decade researching how firms operate, dealing with data swamps before arriving at their core conclusion: "A lot of firm action," they wrote, "is better interpreted as a reflection of the general practices and strategic orientations of the firm 's history," rather than as "the product of a thorough survey of remote decision tree twigs."

And, put in the terminology that people use outside of theoretical economics, it may appear like most businesses make reasonable decisions based on strategic decision-making, but that's not how corporations work at all. Alternatively, companies are driven by long-standing behavioral practices, trends that often arise from thousands of employees' autonomous decisions. And these behaviors have more profound impacts than anyone has ever known.

For example, it may appear like the Chief Executive Officer of a clothing company made a decision last year to include a red cardigan on the catalog cover after carefully analyzing sales and marketing data. Yet, in reality, what really happened was that his vice president regularly bugs blogs devoted to Japanese fashion trends (where red was trendy last spring), and the company's marketers frequently ask their friends which colors are "in," and the company's executives, back from their annual Paris runway show tour, reported learning that designers at rival firms were using new magenta pigments. All these small inputs, the product of uncoordinated interactions between executives talking about rivals and talking to their mates, got mixed up in the more organized research and development routines of the organization before a consensus emerged: Red will be successful this year. No one has made a single, conscious decision. Rather, hundreds of patterns, methods, and behaviors converged until it seemed that red was the inevitable alternative.

Such behavioral habits — or "routines," as Nelson and Winter called them — are incredibly significant, because, without them, most organizations will never get any work done. Routines lay down the hundreds of unwritten laws that businesses need to work. They encourage staff to experiment with new ideas without asking for permission at every step of the way. They have a kind of "organizational memory" so that managers do not have to redesign the selling process every six months or stress every time a VP leaves. Routines minimize uncertainty—a review of earthquake recovery efforts in Mexico and Los Angeles, for example, found that rescue workers' behaviors (which they took from disaster to disaster, and which included issues such as setting up communication networks by employing children to bring messages between neighborhoods) were completely vital, "and without them, the policy formulation was crucial."

Perhaps one of the key benefits of routines is that they allow truces between potentially competing groups or individuals in an organization.

Many analysts are used to seeing businesses as idyllic environments where everyone is committed to a common goal: making as much money as possible. Nelson and Winter have pointed out that this is not how things work in the real world.

Industries aren't large happy families where they all play happily together. In contrast, most workplaces consist of lows where managers fight for power and credit, often in secret skirmishes that improve their success and make their rivals worse. Divisions fight for money and manipulate each other to snatch their glory. Bosses pit their subordinates against each other so that no one may bring up a coup.

Companies are not families. These are battlefields of a civil war.

However, given this potential for internal conflict, most businesses carry out fairly peacefully, year after year, because they have routines — habits — that establish truces that encourage everyone to put aside their rivalries long enough to get a day's work done.

Organizational habits make a simple promise: if you obey existing trends and abide by the agreement, then rivalries will not kill the business, profits will roll in, and finally, everyone will become wealthy. For example, a salesperson knows that she can raise her bonus by offering high discounts to preferred customers in return for larger orders. Yet she also knows that if every salesperson gives away big discounts, the company will go bankrupt, and there won't be any incentives to hand out. Then a pattern emerges: every January, all salespeople come together and decide to restrict how many deals they give in order to protect the profits of the company, and by the end of the year, everybody gets a raise.

Or take a young executive target for a vice president who, with a quiet phone call to a big customer, could ruin the sales and sabotage of a colleague's division, and get him out of the running for promotion. The trouble with manipulation is that even though it's good for you, it's terrible for the company. And, in most corporations, an unspeakable compromise emerges: it's all right to be ambitious, but if you play too hard, your colleagues will come together against you. On the other hand, if you concentrate on improving your own team, rather than weakening your opponent, you 're likely to be taken care of overtime.

Routines and tricks give a kind of rough organizational justice, and because of them, Nelson and Winter wrote, corporate conflict typically follows fairly predictable directions and stays within predictable boundaries that are compatible with the routine... The regular amount of work is completed, reprimands and congratulations are delivered with the regular frequency... No one is trying to direct the or ...

Some of the time, rituals and tricks work well. Rivalries still exist, of course, but due to institutional practices, they are kept within limits, and the company thrives.

Nevertheless, occasionally even a trick proves to be inadequate. Sometimes, as Rhode Island Hospital has found, broken peace can be as devastating as any civil war.

Somewhere in your bedroom, hidden in a desk drawer, there's still a handbook that you got on the first day of work. This includes the types of cost and the rules on vacations, insurance plans, and the organizational chart of the company. It has brightly colored graphs explaining various health insurance plans, a list of appropriate phone numbers, and guidance about how to view or enroll your account in 401(k).

So, imagine what you're going to do to a new boss who asked for advice about how to succeed at your firm. Your suggestions probably won't include anything you'd find in the company's manual. Instead, the tips that you'd go through — who's trustworthy; which secretaries have more clout than their bosses; how to exploit the bureaucracy to do something — are the behaviors that you rely on every day to live. If you could somehow diagram all of your work habits — and the informal power structures, relationships, alliances, and disputes they represent — and then surround your diagram with diagrams prepared by your colleagues, it would create a map of your firm's secret hierarchy, a guide to who knows how to make things happen and who never seems to get ahead of the ball.

Nelson and Winter's routines — and the tricks they make possible — are vital to any kind of enterprise. One study from Utrecht University in the Netherlands, for example, looked at patterns in the world of high fashion. In order to survive, every fashion designer must have some basic skills: imagination and the elegance of haute couture as a start. Yet that isn't enough to succeed. What makes the difference between success or failure is the designer's procedure — whether they have a method for having Italian enough fabric before wholesalers sell it, a process for choosing the right zippers and button sewists, a ten-day, not three-week, procedure for delivering a dress to a shop. Fashion is such a complex industry that, without proper procedures, a new company will get bogged down in logistics, and, as soon as that happens, innovation will cease to matter.

And which of the latest models are most likely to have the right habits? Those who established the right truces and sought the right alliances. Truces are so critical that new fashion brands generally only thrive if they are run by people who have left other fashion companies on good terms.

Others would assume that Nelson and Winter were writing a book on dry economic theory. Yet what they did was a roadmap to success in corporate America.

What're more, Nelson and Winter's hypotheses explain why things went so poorly at Rhode Island Hospital. The hospital had rituals that created an uneasy peace of mind between nurses and doctors — whiteboards, for example, and the messages that nurses whispered to each other were behaviors that formed a simple truce. Such delicate pacts have helped the company to work much of the time. But the tricks are only effective when they build true justice. When a truce is unbalanced — when peace is not real — then procedures always fail when they are most needed.

The crucial problem at Rhode Island Hospital was that the nurses were the only ones who gave up the power to negotiate a truce. It was the nurses who double-checked the patients' medications and made special efforts to write clearly on the charts; the nurses who handled the harassment from the stress-free physicians; the nurses who helped differentiate the compassionate physicians from the despots, so the rest of the staff knew who welcomed the operating room suggestions and who would scream if you opened your mouth. Physicians also did not want to know the names of nurses. "The doctors were in charge, and we were underlings," said one nurse to me. "We tucked our tails and survived."

The tricks at Rhode Island Hospital were one-sided. And, at those vital moments — when, for example, a surgeon was about to make a hasty incision, and a nurse was attempting to intervene — the procedures that would have stopped the incident had crumbled, and the wrong side of an 86 year - older man's head had been opened.

Some may argue that the alternative is more equal. Unless the hospital leadership did a better job of enforcing authority, a stronger balance of power could emerge, and nurses and doctors would be willing to respect each other.

This is a strong start. Sadly, that's not enough. Building effective organizations are not just a matter of managing authority. To order for an organization to succeed, leaders must develop behaviors that establish true and lasting harmony and, paradoxically, make it completely clear who is to charge.

ARE WE RESPONSIBLE FOR OUR HABITS? THE NEUROLOGY OF FREE WILL

The morning started – years before she realized that there were even problems in the first place – Angie Bachmann was at home staring at the Screen, so dull that she was deeply concerned about the reorganization of the silver box.

Her youngest daughter had begun a kindergarten a few weeks ago, and her two older daughters were in high school, their lives overflowing with friends and sports, and their mother's gossip was difficult to understand. Her husband, a land surveyor, frequently left for work at eight o'clock and didn't get home until six o'clock. The building, except for Bachmann, was empty. It was the first time in almost two decades — since she had been married at the age of nineteen and pregnant at the age of twenty, and her days were filled with packing school lunches, playing princess, and driving a family shuttle — that she really felt alone. In high school, her peers told her she was going to be a model — she was so pretty —, but when she dropped out and married a guitar player who eventually got a real job, she wanted to be a mom instead. Now it was in the morning, her three daughters were gone, and Bachmann went — once more — over the kitchen clock to tape a document so as not to look at it for three minutes.

She did not know what to do next.

That day, she made a bargain with herself: if she could make it until noon without going nuts or eating a cake in the refrigerator, she would leave the house and do some fun. She spent the next ninety minutes trying to find out what it was going to be. As the clock reached twelve o'clock, she put on makeup and a comfortable shirt and went to a riverboat casino about twenty minutes away from her home. Also, at noon on Thursday, the casino was packed with people doing tasks, watching soap operas, and doing the laundry. A band was playing near the entrance. There was a guy handing out free drinks. Bachmann ate the shrimp of the buffet. The whole thing seemed comfortable, like playing hooky. She had made her way to a blackjack table where the dealer politely explained the rules. Once her forty dollars of chips were gone, she looked at her watch and saw that two hours had passed, and she had to rush home to pick up her youngest daughter.

That evening at dinner, for the first time in a month, she had plenty to think about as well as a contestant on The Price Is Right.

Angie Bachmann 's father was a truck driver who had made himself a semi-famous songwriter, Midlife. Her uncle was a songwriter, too, and won several awards. On the other hand, Bachmann was often introduced by his parents as "the mother."

"I've always felt like the untalented one," she said to me. "I think I 'm smart, and I know I was a good mom. But there wasn't a lot that I could point to and say, that's why I'm different.

Following the first outing to the casino, Bachmann began going to the riverboat on Friday afternoons once a week. It was a reward for making it through lonely days, keeping the house tidy, keeping it safe. She knew that gambling could lead to trouble, so she set strict rules for herself. Nevermore than one hour per trip at the blackjack table, and she only played what was in her pocket. "I thought it was like a career," she said. "I never left the house before noon, so I've always been home in time to pick up my daughter. I've been really disciplined.

And she's got healthy. At first, she could hardly make her money for the last hour. In six months, though, she had picked up enough tricks to change her rules to accommodate two-or three-hour shifts, and she would still have cash in her pocket when she walked away. One day, she sat down at the blackjack table with $80 in her pocket and walked away with $530—just enough to buy food, pay the phone bill, and put some money in the rainy day fund. Until then, the corporation that owned the casino — Harrah's Entertainment — was sending its vouchers for free buffets. She 'd have a family dinner on Saturday evenings.

The state where Bachmann was gambling, Iowa, had just legalized gambling a few years ago. Prior to 1989, state legislators were concerned that the temptations of cards and dice could be difficult for certain people to avoid. It was a problem as old as the nation itself. Gambling "is the offspring of greed, the brother of iniquity and the father of mischief," wrote George Washington in 1783. "It is a crime that is capable of any imaginable evil .... In a phrase, few benefit from this abominable activity, while thousands are harmed." Protecting people from their bad habits — in reality, determining which habits should be deemed "poor" in the first place — is a prerogative that the legislators have enthusiastically grabbed. Prostitution, gambling, sabbatical liquor sales, prostitution, usury loans, romantic affairs outside marriage (or, if your tastes are uncommon, in marriage) are all practices that various legislators have controlled, prohibited, or sought to prohibit under stringent (and sometimes ineffective) rules.

When Iowa legalized casinos, the lawmakers were so concerned that they restricted the operation to riverboats and ruled that no one should bet more than $5 per bet, with a maximum risk of $200 per person per trip. Within a few years, though, after several state casinos moved to Mississippi where no-limit gambling was permitted, the Iowa legislature repealed those restrictions. In 2010, the state's revenues rose by more than $269 million in gaming taxes.

Around 2000, Angie Bachmann 's parents, both long-term smokers, started to exhibit symptoms of lung disease. She began going to Tennessee to visit them every other week, buying food and helping to prepare dinner. As she returned home to her husband and children, the periods appeared more lonely now. Often the house was quiet all day long; it was as though her friends had refused to invite her to events in her absence, and her family had worked out how to get by on their own.

Bachmann was concerned about her mother, angry that her husband was more interested in her job than in her anxieties, and resentful of her children who did not know that she wanted them now, after all the sacrifices she had made when they were growing up. Yet once she reached the casino, the anxiety would float free. She began a couple of days a week when she didn't visit her parents, and then every Monday, Wednesday, and Friday. She still had rules — but she had been playing for years now, and she understood the axioms that serious players had lived through. She never put a hand down less than $25 and still played two hands at once. "You've got better chances at a higher limit table than at a lower limit table," she said. "You've got to be able to play through tough times before you're lucky. I saw people come in at $150 and win $10,000. I knew I was going to do this if I followed my rules. I was in charge. "1 By then, she didn't have to worry about whether to take another card or double her bet — she was behaving instinctively, just as Eugene Pauly, an amnesiac, had finally learned always to pick the correct cardboard rectangle.

One day in 2000, Bachmann left the casino with $6,000 — enough to pay rent for two months to wipe out the credit card bills stored at the front door. She walked away with $2,000 another day. Often she's lost, but that's part of the training. Good players knew that you had to go down to get back. Finally, Harrah gave her a line of credit so she wouldn't have to bring too much cash. Other players were searching for her out and sitting at her table because she knew what she was doing. The hosts will let her go to the front of the line at the buffet. "I know how to play," she said. "I know it sounds like someone who has a problem not to understand their problem, but the only mistake I made was not to leave. The way I played, there was nothing wrong. As the scale of their gains and losses grew, Bachmann existing laws became steadily more flexible.

One day, she lost $800 in an hour, and then she won $1,200 in forty minutes. But her luck turned around, and she walked away for $4,000. Another day, she lost $3,500 in the morning, won $5,000 by 1 p.m., and lost another $3,000 in the afternoon. The casino had records of how much she owed and earned; she had stopped keeping track of herself. And, for one month, she didn't have enough energy bills in her bank account. She asked her parents for a small loan, and then another one. One month, she borrowed $2,000, the next $2,500. It wasn't a big deal; they were getting the money. Bachmann never had any problems with alcohol or taking medication or overeating.

She was a typical mom, with the same highs and lows like everyone else. And the urge she felt to be gambling — the insistent pull that made her feel depressed or irritable on days when she didn't visit the casino, the way she found herself thinking about it all the time, the thrill she felt on a successful run — took her totally off balance. This was a fresh feeling, so sudden that she didn't realize it was a question until she took care of her life. Upon retrospect, it appeared like there was no dividing line. It was enjoyable one day, and it was uncontrollable the next. She was going to the casino every day by 2001.

She's gone anytime she fights with her husband or feels ignored by her children. She was exhausted and anxious at the tables, all at once, and her anxieties became so faint that she could no longer hear them. The high point of winning was so instant. The agony of losing has gone too quickly. "You want to be a big shot," said her mother when Bachmann called to borrow more money.

"You 're going to keep gambling because you want publicity." Yet that wasn't it.

"I just wanted to feel good about it," she said to me. "It was the first thing I 'd ever done that I seemed to have a talent." In the summer of 2001, Bachmann 's debt to Harrah reached $20,000.

She kept her husband's losses secret, but when her mother eventually cut off her stipends, she broke down and confessed. They hired a bankruptcy attorney, cut off her credit cards, and sat down at the kitchen table to formulate a proposal for a more austere, responsible life. He took her clothes to the used clothing store and withstood the embarrassment of a nineteen-year-old who turned almost all of them down because, he said, they were out of style. Finally, it started to feel like the worst was over.

At last, she thought, the pull was gone.

Yet it wasn't even close to the finish, of course. Years later, after she had lost everything and had destroyed her life and her husband's livelihood after she had thrown away hundreds of thousands of dollars, and her counsel had argued before the highest court of the state that Angie Bachmann was gambling out of habit, not by design, and therefore could not bear responsibility for her losses, after she had become an object of ridicule on the Internet, where people compared her to her.

"I truly believe that someone in my shoes would have done the same thing," Bachmann told me.

On the morning of July 2008, a desperate man on the west coast of Wales took a phone call and called an ambulance operator.

"I think I killed my mom," he said. "Oh, my God, man. I thought someone got in there. I was struggling with the boys, but it was Christine. I must have been a dream or something. What did I do? What did I do? Ten minutes later, police officers came to find Brian Thomas weeping next to his camper truck.

The night before, he explained, he and his wife were sleeping in the car when they were woken up by young men running around the parking lot. They moved their camper to the edge of the field, and they went back to sleep. Then, a few hours later, Thomas woke up to see a man in jeans and a black fleece — one of the racers, he realized, lying on top of his wife. He yelled at the guy, grabbed him by the neck, and tried to pull him off. This was as though he had responded unconsciously. He told the police. The more the man suffered, the easier it was for Thomas to push. The man scratched his arm and attempted to fight back, but Thomas choked, closer and closer, until finally, the man stopped moving. Then Thomas realized that he wasn't a man in his face, but his wife. He lowered her body and started softly nudging her head, attempting to wake her up, asking if she was all right. It's been too late. "I thought someone had come in and strangled her," Thomas told the officers, sobbing.

"This is my country." For the next ten months, when Thomas was in jail pending trial, a portrait of the assassin appeared.

As a boy, Thomas began sleepwalking, often many times a night. He would get out of bed, walk around the house, play toys, or make something to eat, and remember little about what he did the next morning. This was a family joke. Twice a week, it seemed he was going to walk around the yard or someone else's house, all while he was sleeping. This was a habit that his mother would justify when neighbors wondered why her son was walking around their lawns, barefoot, and in his pajamas. When he got older, he would wake up with cuts on his legs with no recollection of where they came from. He swam in the canal once without waking up. Once he had married, his wife was so worried about the risk that he could walk out of the house and into traffic that she locked the door and slept with the keys under her pillow. Every night, the pair would climb into bed and "have a kiss and a cuddle," Thomas said later, and then he would go to his own room and sleep in his own bed. Otherwise, his constant tossing and turning, his shouting and grunting and sporadic wanderings would hold Christine up all night. "Sleepwalking is a reminder that sleep and sleep are not mutually exclusive," said Mark Mahowald, a professor of neurology at the University of Minnesota and a leader in the understanding of sleep habits. "The part of your brain that controls your actions is asleep, but the parts capable of very complex tasks are awake.

The problem is that there's nothing to direct your brain but simple patterns, the most simple behaviors. You do what's in your mind, so you can't make a decision.

By rule, the police had to sue Thomas for the murder. Yet all evidence seemed to show that he and his wife had a happy marriage before that awful night. There was no history of crime. They had two grown daughters and had recently booked a Mediterranean cruise to mark their 40th wedding anniversary. The prosecution called for a sleep specialist —

Dr. Chris Idzikowski of the Edinburgh Sleep Centre — to study Thomas and test the hypothesis that he was unconscious when he murdered his child. During two separate tests, one during Idzikowski's laboratory and the other inside the jail, the researcher used sensors all over Thomas' body and recorded his brain waves, eye movements, chin and leg muscles, nasal airflow, breathing capacity, and oxygen levels while he was unconscious.

Thomas was not the first person to argue that he had committed a crime while asleep, and thus, by implication, could not be held liable for his actions. There is a long tradition of wrongdoers claiming that they are not guilty of "automatism," as sleepwalking and other unconscious activities are identified. And over the last decade, as our perception of the neurology of behaviors and free will has become more complex, these protections have become more convincing. Society, as expressed in our courts and jury, has decided that such patterns are so strong that they overpower our ability to make decisions, and so we are not accountable for what we do.

Sleepwalking is a peculiar outgrowth of the usual way our brains function when we sleep. Much of the time, when our bodies pass in and out of various periods of rest, our much basic neural structure — the brain stem — paralyzes our limbs and nervous system, enabling our minds to perceive hallucinations without our bodies moving about. Typically, people will make a move in and out of paralysis several times a night without any problems. It's known as the "over" in neurology.

Many people's minds, however, are experiencing flipping errors. They go into incomplete paralysis when they sleep, and their bodies become involved when they dream or go through the sleep process. It is the root cause of sleepwalking, and it is an unpleasant but manageable problem for the majority of sufferers. Somebody might dream of eating a cake, for example, and the next morning they'll find a ruined box of doughnuts in the kitchen. Somebody's going to dream of going to the toilet, and then find a wet spot in the corridor. Sleepwalkers can act in complicated ways — for example, and they can open their eyes, see, move about, drive a car or cook a meal — all while basically unconscious, since areas of their brain associated with seeing, walking, driving, and cooking can function when sleeping without feedback from more sophisticated brain regions, such as the prefrontal cortex. Sleepwalkers were known to boil water and make tea. One of them worked a motorboat. Another switched on the electric saw and began to feed in bits of wood before going back to bed. Yet, in general, sleepwalkers are not likely to do things that are dangerous to themselves or anyone. Also, sleeping, there's an impulse to escape danger.

However, when scientists looked at sleepwalker's brains, they found a difference between sleepwalking — in which people would leave their beds and start acting on their dreams or other mild impulses — and anything called sleep terrors. When sleep panic happens, the behavior inside people's brains is significantly different than when they are awake, semi-conscious, or even sleepwalking. Individuals in the midst of sleep terrors tend to be in the grip of awful anxieties, but they don't dream in the usual sense of the word. Their brains shut down, except for the most rudimentary neural regions, which include the so-called "central pattern generators." These brain areas are the same areas studied by Dr. Larry Squire and the MIT scientists who discovered the neurology of the habit loop. In reality, a neurologist sees a brain experiencing sleep terror as very similar to a brain following a habit.

The action of people in the grip of sleep terrors is one of the most primitive behaviors. The "key pattern generators" at work during sleep terror are where behavioral behaviors such as walking, breathing, flinching from loud noise or battling an

175

intruder come from. Typically, we don't think of these behaviors as patterns, but that's what they are: unconscious behaviors so ingrained in our neurology that, according to research, they can occur with almost no feedback from higher regions of the brain.

However, these habits, as they arise during sleep terror, are different in one vital respect: since sleep deactivates the prefrontal cortex and other high-cognition regions when asleep terror habit is activated, there is no chance of conscious intervention. Unless the fight-or-flight habit is accompanied by other high-cognition regions, when the habit of sleep fear is activated, there is no chance of conscious involvement. If the fight-or-flight habit is triggered by sleep panic, there is no possibility that anyone can solve it with logic or justification.

"People with sleep terrors don't dream in the usual sense," said Mahowald, a neurologist. "There are no intricate plots like you because I know from a nightmare. Whether they recall something after that, it's just a picture or emotion — impending disaster, terrible fear, the need to protect themselves, or anyone else.

"Those emotions are very strong, though. These are some of the most important references to all sorts of habits we've learned during our lives. Responding to a threat by running away or protecting ourselves is something that everyone has done since they were children. And when these emotions arise, and the higher brain has no chance of putting things in perspective, we respond to the way our deepest habits tell us. We run or fight or follow whatever behavioral pattern our brains are better suited to.

If someone starts to feel threatened or sexually aroused in the midst of sleep terror — two of the most common sleep terror experiences — they respond by following the patterns associated with these triggers. Persons having sleep terrors jumped off the high roofs as they felt they were escaping from the attackers. They killed their own babies because they claimed they were battling wild animals. They raped their wives, even though their victims begged them to stop, and once the sleepers' anticipation started, they pursued the unconscious practice of fulfilling the impulse. Sleepwalking seems to require some discretion, some intervention of our higher brains that tell us to stay away from the edge of the roof. One in the grip of sleep fear, though, blindly follows the loop of habit no matter where it leads.

Many scientists believe that sleep terrors could be genetic; others claim that disorders such as Parkinson's make them more likely. Its triggers are not well known, but sleep terrors include aggressive impulses for a variety of people. "Sleep terror violence appears to be a response to a real, terrifying picture that can be represented by the person," a group of Swiss researchers wrote in 2009. In people with one form of sleep disorder, "attempt attack of sleeping partners has been reported to occur in 64 percent of cases, with 3 percent injuries."

In both the United States and the United Kingdom, there is a tradition of killers claiming that sleep fear forced them to commit crimes that they would never have done consciously. Four years before Thomas was charged, for example, a man named Jules Lowe was found not guilty of murdering his 83year old father after he argued that the attack had taken place during a sleep terror. The plaintiffs argued that it was "far-fetched to the extreme" to conclude that Lowe was unconscious while punching, kicking, and stamping his father for more than twenty minutes, leaving him with more than ninety injuries. The jury did not consent and set him free. In September 2008, 33-year-old Donna Sheppard-Saunders nearly suffocated her mother by putting a pillow over her face for thirty seconds. She was later absolved of the attempted murder by claiming that she had behaved when she was sleeping. In 2009, a British soldier confessed to raping a teenage girl but said he was asleep and unconscious while undressing, pulling down her underwear, and beginning to have sex. As he woke up, mid-rape, he apologized and called the police. "I've just done some kind of felony," he said to the 911 operator. "I just don't know what's going on. I ended up on top of her. "He had a history of sleep deprivation and was found not guilty. More than 150 murderers and rapists have avoided punishment in the last century through automated security. Judges and jury members, speaking on behalf of society, said that since the criminals did not want to commit their crimes — because they did not knowingly participate in the violence — they could not bear the blame.

Brian Thomas also saw it as a case where poor sleep, rather than a violent instinct, was at fault. "I will never forgive myself," he said to one of the lawyers. "Why did I do that? After Dr. Idzikowski, a sleep specialist, examined Thomas in his laboratory, he reported his findings: Thomas was sleeping when he killed his wife.

He had not committed a felony knowingly. When the trial began, prosecutors presented their facts to the jury.

Thomas had confessed to murdering his wife, the jurors said. He realized that he had a history of sleepwalking. His inability to take precautions while on vacation, they said, made him responsible for his crime. But as proceedings progressed, it was apparent that prosecutors were fighting an uphill battle.

Thomas's lawyer argued that his client didn't intend to kill his wife — in reality, that night, he wasn't in control of his own behavior. Instead, he responded instinctively to the perceived threat. He had a habit almost as old as our species: an instinct to fight an intruder and defend a loved one. If the most primitive parts of his brain had been exposed to the cue — somebody strangling his wife — his reflex had taken over, and he had fought back, with no chance of his higher cognition interceding. Thomas was guilty of nothing more than being human, the lawyer claimed and behaving in the way that his neurology — and most primal habits — forced him to behave. Also, the prosecution's own witnesses appeared to support the defense.

While Thomas believed he was capable of sleepwalking, the prosecution's own therapists claimed, there was little to indicate to him that it was actually probable that he would be killed. He 'd never hurt someone in his sleep before. He had never hurt his wife before. As the chief psychiatrist of the prosecution took the stand, Thomas 's counsel began his cross-examination.

Does it seem fair that Thomas was to be found guilty of an act that he did not realize would happen?

In her view, Dr. Caroline Jacob said that Thomas could not fairly have expected his crime.

And if he was convicted and sentenced to Broadmoor Prison, where some of Britain's most violent and mentally disturbed inmates were held, well, "he doesn't belong there." The next morning, the Chief Prosecutor informed the jury.

"At the time of the crime, the defendant was unconscious, and his mind had no power of what his body was doing," he said.

"We have come to the conclusion that the public interest can no longer be served by trying to seek a special decision from you. They, therefore, will not give any more evidence and allow you to return a straight, not guilty verdict. "The jury did so. Before Thomas was released, the judge said to him, "You are a good man and a faithful husband.

I strongly suspect that you might well have a feeling of remorse. You have no liability in the eyes of the law. You 're being released. This seems to be a rational outcome.

Thomas was clearly devastated by his crime, after all. He had no idea what he was doing when he acted — he was merely pursuing a pattern, and his decision-making ability was, in effect, incapacitated. Thomas is the most forgiving killer possible, someone, so similar to becoming a survivor himself that the judge wanted to comfort him when the trial ended. And many of the same reasons can be made for Angie Bachmann, the gambler.

She was saddened by her actions, too. Afterward, she will say she has a strong sense of remorse. And as it turns out, she often pursued profoundly rooted patterns that made it extremely difficult for decision-making to interfere. But in the eyes of the law, Bachmann is liable for her behavior, and Thomas is not.

Is it true that Bachmann, a gambler, is more guilty than Thomas, a murderer? How does this teach us about the ethics of habit and choice? Three years after Angie Bachmann declared bankruptcy, her father died.

She had spent the previous half-decade moving between her home and her parents' house, taking care of them as they became increasingly sick. His death was a shock to him. Then her mother died two months later. "My whole life has disintegrated," she said.

"I would wake up every morning, and for a second, forget that they had passed away, and then it would rush to the point that they were gone, and I would feel like someone was standing on my face. I couldn't think about anything else. Once I got out of bed, I didn't know what to do.

As their wills were read, Bachmann discovered that she had inherited nearly $ 1 million.

She used $275,000 to buy her family a new home in Tennessee, near where her mother and father had died, and she spent a little more to move her grown daughters nearby so that they were all together. Casino gambling wasn't legal in Tennessee, and "I didn't want to fall back into bad habits," she told me. "I wanted to stay away from something that reminded me of feeling out of reach." She changed her phone numbers and didn't tell the casinos her new address. This way, it felt better.

Then one night, driving through her old hometown with her husband, taking the last piece of furniture from her former home, she started thinking about her father. What would she have done without them? Why wasn't she a better daughter? She began to hyperventilate. It felt like the beginning of a panic attack. She had been gambling for years, but at that moment, she felt like she had to do something to take her mind off the pain. She was looking at her friend. She's been busy. This was a one-time matter.

"Let's get to the casino," she said.

As they came in, one of the managers remembered her as she was a regular and welcomed her to the players' lounge. He asked how she had been, and it was all tumbling out: the death of her mother, and how hard she had been hit, how tired she had been all the time, how she felt like she was on the verge of collapse. The boss was a really good listener. It was so good to finally say what she had been feeling and to realize that it was natural to feel this way.

She sat down at the blackjack table and played for three hours. The fear melted into background noise for the first time in months. She knew how to do it. She's gone blank. She's lost a few thousand dollars.

Harrah's Entertainment — the corporation that owned the casino — was known to the gaming industry for the complexity of its consumer monitoring systems. Computer programs were at the heart of the scheme, just like those developed by Andrew Pole at Target, predictive algorithms that analyzed gambling patterns and tried to find out how to persuade people to spend more. The company assigned players a "projected lifetime value" and software designed calendars that projected how much they would visit and how much they would spend. The company monitored consumers through loyalty cards and mailed coupons for free meals and cash vouchers; telemarketers called people home to inquire where they were. Casino workers were prepared to inspire guests to discuss their lives, in the hope that they could share details that could be used to determine how much they had to play with. One of Harrah 's executives called this "Pavlovian Advertising" strategy. The company carried out thousands of experiments every year to refine their methods. Customer monitoring boosted the company's revenues by billions of dollars and was so precise that it could track the player 's spending to one cent and one minute.

Of course, Harrah realized that a few years ago, Bachmann declared bankruptcy and went free from $20,000 in gambling debt. Yet shortly after she had spoken to the casino manager, she started to receive phone calls from free limos that would drive her to Mississippi casinos. They decided to take her, and her husband to Lake Tahoe, put them in a hotel, and give them tickets to the Eagles show. "I said my daughter had to come, and she was going to bring a friend," Bachmann said. There was no question, the company answered. The airfare and the rooms were free. She sat in the front row at the concert. Harrah gave her $10,000 to play with the house compliments.

The deals were already flowing. Each week, another casino called, asking if she needed a limo, entry to the shows, a plane ticket. At first, Bachmann refused, but gradually she started to say yes any time an invitation came. Once a family friend decided she wanted to get married in Las Vegas, Bachmann made a phone call, and they were in the Palazzo the next day. "Not too many people really know it exists," she told me. "I called and asked about it, and the operator said it was too confidential to send out details on the phone. There was something out of the movie in the house. There were six bedrooms and a deck and a private hot tub for each room. I've got a butler.

Once she went to the casinos, just as soon as she walked in, her gambling habits took over. She would also have practiced a game for hours. At first, she started tiny, using only the money of the casino. Instead, the numbers got higher, and she was going to load up her chips with withdrawals from the ATM. It didn't seem to her that there was a question. Finally, she played $200 to $300 a player, two hands at a time, often for a dozen hours at a time. She won $60,000 one night. She walked away two times, up to $40,000. One time she went to Vegas with $100,000 in her pocket, and she came home with nothing. This didn't affect her way of life. Her bank account was still so large that she never had to think about finances. That's why her parents had given her an inheritance in the first place: so she could enjoy herself.

She would try to slow down, but the appeals of the casino became more insistent. "One host told me he 'd get fired if I didn't come that weekend," she said. "They'd say, 'We sent you to this concert, and we've given you this lovely space, and you haven't played that much lately.' Well, they've done those nice things for me."

Her husband's grandma died in 2005, and the family went back to her old hometown for a funeral. The night before the service, she went to the casino to clear her mind and get emotionally prepared for all the action the next day. In the course of twelve hours, she lost $250,000. At the time, it was almost as though the size of the loss had not been reported. As she thought about it later — a quarter of a million dollars gone — it didn't seem possible. She had always been lying to herself about too much: that her marriage was happy because she and her husband often went days without even speaking; that her friends were nearby because she realized that they were on trips to Vegas and were gone when it was over; that she was a good mom when she saw her daughters make the same mistakes that she had made, getting pregnant too early; that her parents should have been pregnant too long. It seemed like there were only two choices: to continue lying to herself or to accept that she had dishonored everything her mother and father had worked so hard to gain.

That's a quarter of a million dollars. She didn't say anything to her friend. "I've been concentrating on something different every night that pops into my head," she said.

Soon, however, the losses were too great to disregard. Some nights after her husband was asleep, Bachmann would crawl out of bed, sit down at the kitchen table, and scribble out estimates, trying to make sense of how far he had gone. The depression that started after the death of her parents seemed to have deepened. She had been feeling so drained all the time.

And Harrah kept calling.

"This struggle begins when you know how much you've lost, and then you feel like you can't stop because you've got to get it back," she said. "Sometimes I'd begin to feel jumpy like I couldn't think straight, and I'd realize that if I were to believe that I could make another trip soon, it would calm me down. Then they would call, and I would say yes because it was too easy to give in. I always did feel that I could take it back. I should have won then. If you couldn't win, gambling wouldn't be legal, wouldn't it? In 2010, the cognitive neuroscientist Reza Habib asked twenty-two men to lie inside the MRI and watch a slot machine turn around and around.

Half of the participants were "pathological gamblers"—people who had lied to their families about gambling lost a job at gambling or rebounded at a casino — while the other half were people who played socially but did not exhibit any risky conduct. Everyone was placed on their backs inside a narrow tube and asked them to look around a video screen at the wheels of lucky 7s, apples, and gold bars. The slot machine had three outcomes: a victory, a loss, and a near-miss, in which the slots nearly matched but could not suit at the last moment. None of the participants had any money won or lost. They had to watch the screen while the MRI recorded its neurological activity. "In particular, we were interested in looking at the brain processes involved in habits and addictions," Habib told me. "We found that the addictive players in neurology were more passionate about winning.As symbols were lined up, even if they didn't actually earn any money, their emotional and reward-linked brains were much more involved than non-pathological players.

"But the surrounding misses were also surprising. Near misses felt like wins for pathological gamblers. Their brains reacted much as they did. For a nonpathological player, however, an almost miss was a loss. Those who do not have problems with gambling know better that a close miss means you are actually failing.

Two groups saw the same thing, but from a psychological point of view, they interpreted it differently. Those with gambling problems are given a mental boost from near misses — which is presumably why Habib hypothesizes they are playing so long as anybody else: that close missing motivates certain habits to make another bet. When they saw a miss, the nonproblem gamblers got a dose of anxiety that triggered a different habit, which means I should quit before things get worse. It's not clear if problem gamblers' brains are different because they're born that way, or whether repeated exposure to slot machines, online poker, and casinos will affect how the brain works. What is obvious is that actual neurological variations have an effect on how pathological players interpret information — which helps explain why Angie Bachmann has lost control every time she visits a casino. Gaming firms are well aware of this trend, of course, which is why, in the last decades, slot machines have been reprogrammed to produce a more consistent stream of near-wins. 3 Gamblers who keep betting on close wins are what makes casinos, racetracks, and state lotteries so lucrative. "Adding a near miss to a lottery is like pouring jet fuel on a spark," said a state lottery expert who talked to me under anonymity. "Do you want to know why the profits have exploded? Any other scratch-off ticket is built to make you feel like you've almost won.

The areas of the brain Habib scrutinized in his experiment — basal ganglia and brain stem — are the same areas where patterns exist (as well as where sleep terror behaviors begin). In the last decade, as new groups of pharmaceuticals have arisen to address the region — such as Parkinson's disease drugs — we've learned a lot about how sensitive those external stimulus patterns can be. Class action cases have been brought against drug makers in the United States, Australia, and Canada, claiming that pharmaceuticals have induced patients to gamble, eat, shop, and masturbate by manipulating the circuits involved in the habit process. In 2008, a federal jury in Minnesota awarded a patient $8.2 million in a case against a drug manufacturer after the man alleged that his drugs had caused him to gamble more than $250,000 away. Hundreds of these cases are pending.

"In those situations, we can certainly assume that patients have no influence over their obsessions, as we can point to a drug that affects their neurochemistry," Habib said. "So when we look at the minds of people who are obsessive gamblers, they look very similar — except they can't blame meds for that. They tell researchers that they don't want to gamble, but they can't stop the cravings. And why do we assume that these gamblers are in charge of their acts, and Parkinson 's patients are not? Angie Bachmann went to the casino on 18 March 2006 at Harrah 's invitation.

Her bank account was nearly empty by then. As she tried to quantify how much she 'd lose in her lifetime, she put the number at around $900,000. She had told Harrah that she was almost finished, but the man on the phone said he was coming. They 'd give her a line of credit, he said.

"It felt like I couldn't say no, that any time they dangled the slightest threat in front of me, my brain would shut down. I know it sounds like an excuse, but they've always said it would be different this time, and I knew no matter how hard I fought against it, I was finally going to give in.

She brought with her the last of her assets. She began to play $400 a hand, two hands at a time. When she could get up a little, she would say, just $100,000, and she could stop and have something to give to her children. Her husband joined her for a bit, but he went to bed at midnight. About 2 A.M., the money with which she had come was gone. The Harrah employee gave her a pledge note to sign. She signed six times for more cash, for a total of $125,000.

She reached a hot streak at about six o'clock in the morning, and her piles of chips began to rise. A crowd has gathered. She did a fast tally: not enough to pay off the notes she 'd taken, but if she kept playing smart, she 'd come out on top, and then quit for good. She's won five times in a row. She just had to win $20,000 more to get ahead. The dealer hit 21. He hit it again, then. A few hands later, he hit it for the third time. At ten o'clock in the morning, all her chips were gone. She asked for more cash, but she said no to the casino.

Bachmann left the table dazed and headed back to her room. It sounded as though the floor was trembling. She traced her hand along the wall so that if she fell, she would know which way to lean. Her husband was waiting for her when she got to the house.

"It's all gone," she said.

"Why don't you just take a shower and go to bed? "He said that. "It's all right. You've lost it before.

"It's all gone now," she said.

"What do you mean by that? "The money has gone," she said.

"It's all." "We still have the building, at least," he said.

She didn't tell him that she had taken out a line of credit from her home months earlier and had played it down.

HOW TO UNDERSTAND PASSIVE INCOME OPPORTUNITIES

"Make money when you sleep" has a nice ring, doesn't it? After all, one of the objectives of financial freedom is to create wealth that doesn't take your time, so you can enjoy life and do the things you want to do.

The fact is, creating a passive income stream is typically not passive at all. It needs time, energy, expertise, or all three of them. But where are you going to start? The first step is to create small egg savings account for the nest that you can use for later. We 're going to come back to this.

Multiple streams of passive revenue have an additional short-term benefit: it can make you stronger and more capable of confronting economic shocks.

Passive income is a long-term option requiring short-term trade. If you are able to dedicate your time to the following steps and ideas for years to come, you will learn quickly.

You just have to decide where to go and evaluate what money you 're willing to spend on your passive income ideas.

I will cut passive revenue and show you what I've done to create my passive revenue streams, so you can if you want to get the ideas right. Let's just dive in! Just dive in!

Passive income means money obtained with minimal involvement in any undertaking, which requires little daily effort or attention on the part of the person.

Let's break that down a bit more:

✓ Passive — requiring little or no of your most valuable resource, your energy!

✓ Income-generating cash inflows to you that either reflects money that you use in your everyday life, or that you re-invest.

A successful move is to be able to get a full-time job, which takes a lot of your working time and still run your passive income streams.

Passive income golden rule – secure your time.

More money than anything else is passive profit. You can do a lot to make money, but not all sources of income are passive. I am all about developing a company or a side hustle actively, but for the income to be genuinely passive, it must take increasingly less effort to generate profit, and ultimately no effort is needed (or very little effort to maintain).

For instance, if you need two hours to make 100 dollars today, and it takes two hours to make 100 dollars next week or a year, then it's not a passive revenue stream, because it takes the same effort (money, time, etc.).

On the other hand, if I open an investment account today, it will take some effort. Yet as that account expands, and I review it four times a year, my returns go up, and my effort goes down.

Same if I'm trying to create an online course. At first, I don't make much money, and my commitment is very high. But first, I 'm spending a lot of energy. When the course is complete, I do some continuing marketing and customer service, which amounts to only a few hours a week, with sales going on month after month.

Can you get a picture? Then let's think about what passive income isn't.

WHAT PASSIVE INCOME IS NOT

Your job

Clearly, the entire purpose of passive income is to offset, raise, or get you out of work so that you can retire, travel, or spend more time with your loved ones.

Side hustles.

Side hustles are a fantastic way to make money, but not all side hustles are passive. Side hustles are typically aggressive, and maybe with systemization, they will transform into passive revenue streams.

If you intend to continue spending the same (or more) amount of time for the same amount of financial products, the company is not passive. Be careful here, because note, at first, that a passive income stream may require more time, energy, or work than it produces. You need to assess the passive income potential for you in its long-term condition.

Consulting

Consulting is just another work – ideal for a side hustle, but not just passive. To order to be passive to consulting, you would need to develop a relationship with other people and finally be able to move away from work.

Investing for speculation

Here's where I break my head. I do not believe that capital appreciation savings are just passive profits. Why? Since stock appreciation is not income. On the other hand, investing in stable companies that disburse cash in the form of dividends is definitely a passive income strategy. The question is, are you getting cash back, or are you just going to see the return if you sell the investment?

Investments like cryptocurrencies and commodities are also reserved for price speculation. There are also occasions when these assets can be allocated some of your portfolios, but investing like this is not a secure passive income strategy.

How To Start Building Passive Income

There's no magic trick that turns your time into money. Alternatively, you plant seeds so that your money grows even while you're sleeping or walking your dog in the park.

You will spend $100 on the initial downtime you bring into passive income as complicated as beginning a blog or signing into a Robo consulting program. If you are a businessman with a great business plan, a creative artist, or just extra cash to spend, you will earn passive income.

1. Start building a nest egg

Recall earlier when I said that you needed to create passive income on time, money, or skills? Let your money start. Let's start your money. Open an account for high-interest savings and park $100. You only made a passive profit, boom! It might not be much, but you will be earning interest on it, and many online banks now offer cash incentives for opening their accounts. Right now, the CIT branch is our favorite.

2. Assess your skills

I was a licensed financial planner before I started Goodfinancialcents.com to broaden my business and fix unique client issues. I realized that I could use these skills to build amazing content online and that I could make money from this blog over time.

I've got friends who were stock traders who now have groups around the expertise or write for financial publications. Some friends have been successful bosses, and now they're creating career websites.

What the heck are you good at? Who the heck are you crazy about? Take a short inventory and discover how others have used those skills to create income streams.

3. Measure your time, your resources, and your commitment. Make your commitments realistic.

Time is a tough one because it's our finite commodity. To try to make more money or create passive income can be a trap because it normally requires you to learn new subjects or skills. Remember, you may have to bite the bullet in the short term, but in the long run, your goal is to reduce your investment in time.

Are you fully committed to this? A lot of time is spent on current work, family, and social activities. If you don't have a lot of time, you'll need to lean more towards investing or getting someone else to do a job for you.

In this guide, we have labeled each idea with an effort level (1-5, 5 is the most demanding), so that you adapt your existing skills to the idea.

4. Ideate and choose

The last step is to put some ideas on paper and to decide how to start. We have created the list below to help you get your idea started. We've created this list of ideas to help you get started. Your riches and independence are here!

PASSIVE INCOME IDEAS

Generate Cash Investment Revenue

1. REAL ESTATE EMPIRE FROM YOUR COUCH.

Real estate has long been a source of wealth development. Investment in real estate took a lot of time, energy, and expertise. Immobilien investment applications, however, have democratized access to the asset class – which makes it easier for me and you to produce passive non-work income.

Below are the tools to search if you are interested in:

Fundraise

Fundraise is specialized in trusts for Immobiliare investment (REITs). Whether you live in an expensive city or have no time to run a house, REITs are the way to go.

REIT owns, operates, and distributes income-producing assets to its creditors. REIT investments were costly and required to be accredited, but all this was changed by Fundraise.

The Fundrise minimum investment is just $500.

Roofstock

Roofstock is a marketplace for sales of turnkey single-family homes. The word "turnkey" means that the numbers have been split, the house should have been restored, and the tenants could already be included!

As an investor, all you have to do is get the cash. When you buy a home, it's 100% yours, and the rental income goes directly to you.

RealtyMogul

I recommend checking out RealtyMogul for something between Fundrise's REITs and Roofstock's single-family homes.

Realty Mogul is a crowdfunding site that pools investors' money to buy big-ticket assets (office buildings, retail space, etc.). The minimum amount of investment is $5,000.

2. PEER TO PEER LENDING

Peer-to-peer lending, or P2P lending, is my preference. The aim is to lend money to individuals or companies. They'll pay you back, plus interest.

Let's assume that someone has to borrow 10k dollars to raise their debt. They set up an account with the Lending Club (for example), and, depending on their credit history, income, etc., they are granted an interest rate on loan. The investor (you) also creates an account with the Lending Club and purchases the debt. When the creditor makes monthly contributions, you will be paying the principal and interest on your Lending Club investment account.

There are several companies that underwrite P2P loans, some like the Lending Club, which facilitates personal loans, while others, like Worthy, facilitate business loans (the process is exactly the same).

Expected returns are within the 5% range (depending on the platform and type of loan). Although not necessarily stock returns, 5% or more is better than most national bank interest rates.

3. INVEST IN HIGH-YIELD SAVINGS

Savings accounts may be the most boring investment ever made, but they are also the safest.

At 0.15 percent interest or lower, you would need to exceed the FDIC-insured limit of $250,000 to see any real action.

However, Online savings accounts are far faster than regular banks. Better yet, these rates competed for CD rates without having been locked into your money for several years.

CIT Bank is our favorite savings account choice at present.

4. INVEST IN THE MARKETS, PASSIVELY

The most effective way of building long-term income and wealth is to invest in stocks and bonds through private pensions or brokerage accounts. However, the data are very good that the average citizen like you and I have to invest passively through cheap ETFs and index funds.

You can do so in two ways:

Set it and forget it with a Robo-advisor

It is as passive as you can to let an algorithm handle your investments. Robo consultants like Betterment allow you to define your willingness to risk and then sit back and allow your income to flow. And the rates are far lower than what a contractor should have charged. Below is a list of some of the leading robot consulting websites.

I was a long-standing supporter of Betterment, and in my Betterment Investment Analytical, I even interviewed their CEO. Improving your investment taxes is critical, and they work with you to provide you with the best financial advice that their algorithms.

Unlike other Robo consultants, Betterment allows you to speak to a human if you wish. Betterment pays the same rates as Wealthfront, but won't exempt your first $10,000 fee.

Choose your own online trading dividend stocks or ETFs.

You can generate regular reactive earnings at an annualized rate that is much higher than what you get from bank investments by building a portfolio of high-dividend stocks.

Equally significant is the potential for capital appreciation because stocks are high in dividends. It helps you to receive passive income from two sources – dividends and capital gains.

By opening an account with any of the following brokerages, you can make this process very simple and cost-effective. Most brokerages are currently no longer charging trading commissions, which is a big saving for us!

Online brokerages provide you with a little more flexibility and choose which ETFs you want to invest in (and in each stock). Online nominee brokers such as TD Ameritrade and E-trade have done very well with low stock and bond transaction fees.

However, M1 Finance is currently my favorite online broker. They make it super easy to make passive investments in ETFs and complete their service portfolio to give you seamless access to your capital.

5. INVEST IN CDS

CDs are easy, simple, and far from the most interesting investment strategy out there, if I am honest. Yet if you want to make money while you sleep, nothing is more passive than CDs. Investing in a deposit certificate is a low-risk interest-free solution.

The CDs are like a bank account for fishing. You can't spend your money until it matures, which is decided by the time you open your account. This period can vary between months and years.

Be sure to buy your CD (up to $250k is insured) from FDIC's insured financial institution to get the best CD rates. The longer the CD runs, the more leverage the financial institution has to pay.

GENERATE PASSIVE TIME INVESTMENT PROFITS

1. START A BLOG

It is the key reason I finally created my family's passive income – I started the good finance centers! Blogs are an unbelievable source of passive revenue. But more than just posting good stuff, there is to make a blog fund.

You may want to take a minute and prepare to start a blog if you are looking for an incredibly inexpensive but highly scalable way to make cash flow for yourself.

Did you know: you can start your first month's blog for as little as one cent and a few dollars a month thereafter?

Here is the idea: if you can make a lot of value for many people regularly using your blog, you can make an incredible amount of passive income. By posting to your blog more and more, your website will begin to attract traffic, whether you spend extra time or not.

Which is catch here? What is catch here? It takes time to get things going. It takes time. That's it. The earlier you begin, the sooner the income stream develops.

You may want to participate in our Make 1k Challenge, a free email course that takes you through the first steps to start and make your first $1,000 blog.

The first move is to register a domain and pick a blog hosting contract.

2. CREATE AN ONLINE COURSE OR GUIDE

Online learning is a flourishing business opportunity. You can set up a course on just about everything. How to tie a fishing knot, how to clean cats, how to talk to girls (or boys)—it's all there. My friend Holly has a successful career in becoming a freelance writer.

How?

One very easy way to do this is to create and share your curriculum is Teachable.com. Teachable has over three million students, and it's a great way to get your content in front of others.

What are you putting in your online course? Good question, man. You can add the following:

- ✓ Appropriate video lessons.

- ✓ Please accept checklists for the completion of the steps that you recommend in your video lessons.

- ✓ Relevant little ebooks to accompany the lessons.

- ✓ Appoint audio files for people listening while they're on the road.

- ✓ Appropriate informative interviews with like-minded experts.

- ✓ A whole lot more!

Pro Tip: Create multiple packages at different price points. Some people want it all so that you can have 'plays' at the highest price point and have two lower price points so that you can have the greatest possible number of orders.

Try making an online guide if you do not write articles or create videos, and you want to make money online. SecurityGuardTrainingHQ.com Pat Flynn 's website is a great example of this revenue stream. On this website, the map enables us to click on every state to see the safety guard requirements for that state.

You can make money from other devices, such as Google AdSense, sponsors, and even memberships in your online guide, by offering comprehensive details in a guide-like format.

It's a brilliant idea!

3. SELL AN E-BOOK

I wrote Soldier of Finance to constantly support my clients and others with the same financial difficulties. Though not technically an ebook, Kindle, and paperback are also available, this book always gives me a passive income many years after I publish it.

4. SELL STOCK PHOTOS

Are you a photographer or someone who enjoys snapping a picture? Put your talent to use! If you want to make some extra money for your images, you might consider selling your images as a stock photo. The best way to make your photographs available for sale as a stock image is to use a third-party platform, such as Adobe Stock, Shutterstock, Alamy, etc.

If you have the expertise and tools to do so, you can also be able to sell your stock photos on your own website.

5. BECOME A SOCIAL MEDIA INFLUENCER

Do you know that you can get paid for social media posting? There are a variety of ways to make money as a social media influencer. You will partner with businesses to create supported posts/content that the client would pay for. Typically, the rates for sponsored posts are calculated by the number of followers you have and the rate of your engagement. You may also gain money by posting affiliate links, writing blog posts, or organizing events / participating in events as an influencer. To start making money as a social media influencer, it's a smart idea to create a marketing kit that highlights your social marketing pages, your niche, and examples of your work.

SEMI-PASSIVE SIDE HUSTLES

1. Deliver for Instacart

If you are looking for a versatile way to make extra money, Instacart is a great alternative. Instacart is an online supermarket company that partners with local grocery stores to deliver food to your door. As an Instacart employee, you will shop for the products at the grocery store and then deliver the goods to the customer's door. Today, demand for Instacart shoppers is higher than ever before.

As a shopper, you would be paid on a weekly basis, have the freedom to pick your own hours, possibly have the chance to receive tips, and be eligible for special earnings promotions.

Instacart has also launched a range of new features recently, including contactless communication and recording of accidents.

2. Deliver for Postmates

Postmates is a goods and food distribution center that allows customers to order almost anything they want, such as personal items, grocery stores, and restaurant meals.

It's 100 percent free to sign up for delivery to Postmates and Postmates to pick up 100 percent of what they earn every time they complete the delivery.

Postmates deliveries drive love flexibility and independence to work whenever they want. Postmates offers a weekly payout and a super simple onboarding process.

3. Rent Your Car

It used to seem strange to rent a spare room to a stranger, or to stay at a stranger's home when you're on vacation. Thanks to the likes of Airbnb and others, these sharing economy services have shown us that it's not that scary!

So let me ask, how do you feel about renting out your car?

Think about that. Think about that. Car rental agencies are too expensive to deal with (Enterprise, Notice, Budget, etc.).

The industry was disrupted by an undertaking named Turo, just as Airbnb disrupted the hotel industry. People all over the country make money by renting their cars to foreigners.

If you're not using your car for a few days, or if you have a spare one, just enter Turo's free platform, list your vehicle, and charge whatever you want for the day.

4. Get Paid For Your Opinion

Do you know that you can get paid for taking online surveys? Right from the comfort of your sofa, you could make money by surfing the internet. There are lots of fantastic survey sites out there, and some of them give you a bonus just to sign up.

5. Network Marketing

Network marketing is a business model for independent contractors to buy into a company. They earn a commission on the products they sell. Many individuals are drawn to network marketing as this field allows them to be their own boss, to set their own hours, and to be flexible.

There are a lot of network marketing firms out there. Some of the most popular companies are Mary Kay, DoTerra, Pampered Chef, and Rodan & Fields.

There are a few different ways to make money from network marketing. You can make a profit by selling the company 's goods with others, you can use the goods yourself, and you can recruit others.

TOOLS TO HELP OUTSOURCE YOUR BUSINESS

If you currently own a company, outsourcing will free up your time so that you can concentrate on other activities that will result in more sales. If you don't want to recruit staff, try recruiting freelancers who work as contract workers. Look for freelancers with a good work ethic that delivers quality results.

Here are the companies that I recommend starting with:

- ✓ CloudPeeps: CloudPeeps does an outstanding job matching company in need with professional, seasoned freelancers who can handle anything from PR and marketing to web creation and administrative tasks.

- ✓ Fiverr: Fiverr has it all. Like CloudPeeps, it provides hand-picked freelancers for all your business needs.

- ✓ Guru provides similar services to Fiverr and CloudPeeps but emphasizes their flexible payment choices, such as hourly pay, monthly payments, milestone payments, and project payments.

- ✓ PeoplePerHour: With an innovative AI program that suits your project requirements to be a great freelancer and appearances on Forbes, CNBC, and BBC, PeoplePerHour provides a genuine pool of talented artists to outsource to.

✓ Upwork: Like other freelancing networks, Upwork pairs you with freelancers in a number of sectors and boasts hiring by companies like Microsoft, with short-term, full-time, and recurring options.

HOW CAN I GENERATE PASSIVE INCOME?

Passive income will work for you, regardless of whether you have millions of dollars to spend and little time to spare, or $0, enough free time, and a spark of creativity.

Although they could take some capital and fortitude to get going, the money makers on this list will continue to make money for you long after you've been on the job.

So look at what you're working with: set your financial goals and determine how much time, energy, and money you 're willing to put into your company.

Whether you choose to invest, buy a business, outsource your own, or get paid for your daily routine, you can thrive on passive earnings.

What the heck are you waiting for? Plant the seeds with one of the ideas on the list today.

HOW TO BE SMART WITH YOUR MONEY

A major part of winning life is learning the wisdom of money because money affects almost everything that we do in our modern society.

When you know how to be wise about your money and handle it well, you 're going to be able to do some great things in life, such as creating wealth, so you can have protection and do the things you love doing, living in comfort, helping those in need, supporting worthy causes, and more.

TIPS FOR HOW TO BE SMART WITH MONEY

1. Determine your why and set financial goals.

The very first thing I think you 're supposed to do when you want to be smart about your money is to figure out why you're financial. Why do you want to change your financial situation? Why do you believe you need to pay off your debt or start saving more money or investing in retirement? What are your main financial objectives and dreams?

Your reason is crucial because it will motivate you to set crucial financial goals that will change your life's trajectory. With simple, realistic, but stunning, far-reaching financial goals, you 're going to be able to do amazing things with your money that most people will never do. It's sad, but it's real.

A lot of people go through life half-awake, never having the drive or discipline or determination to really do awesome things. But you're not the same person! Or if you were, you 're no longer there!

You 're going to do amazing things in your life by setting and constantly working towards easy but ambitious financial goals, including building emergency savings and high costs, getting out of debt (including paying off that mortgage!), investing in retirement. Helping you pay for your children's college education so that they won't be saddled with debt, and building wealth so that you can achieve ultimate financial freedom.

2. Make a spending plan.

After you've determined your financial reasoning, get on with it by developing a strategy to achieve your financial objectives — a financial strategy better known as the budget. So either tag it a spending plan or a smart money plan or whatever you want if you don't love the word b.

When you set up your budget, make it a zero-based budget. In other words, you don't assign your monthly salary to something on paper. You might think that this seems odd; that it would be better to leave a little money as a buffer. And that's perfect if you call the money to be placed into a particular savings account or anything like your emergency fund. But don't just leave your money unaccounted for. The explanation for that? It's almost inevitable that we're going to get wasted.

3. Differentiate needs versus wants to ensure you are smart with your money.

As you create your budget, start making a difference between needs and wants, and make adjustments to your budget as you go along. Sometimes, we 're doing a pretty good job of justifying wants by calling them needs. But to really separate needs from wants, consider this: you need accommodation (unless you can live under a palm tree or something), but you don't really need a fancy or a new or even a decent house.

You also need food, but you don't need restaurant food or gourmet food, or you always need to eat brand-name food. You need to travel, but you can be able to get around with one car for a while (or maybe no car if you can use bikes or your feet or public transport). And you certainly don't need a brand-new or ultra-safe or super-stylish vehicle.

The more you can distinguish between needs and desires, and first base your budget on your needs, and then the more you can actually afford while still saving and spending appropriately to achieve long-term, important financial goals, the happier you will be financially later in life.

When you build your monthly spending plan or budget, first assign money to your needs. That means first designating money for fair food, clothes, housing, transportation, utilities, and other real needs.

Designate resources to set up a sufficient (three-to six-month; I suggest six-month) emergency fund, construct sinking funds to cover potential larger expenses and larger purchases (such as apps and so on) and have appropriate retirement savings (save at least ten but preferably 15% of your retirement income as soon as you are financially able to do so).

4. See where you can reduce your spending to be smarter with your money.

To be smarter about your money and meet your financial goals, you 're likely to need to popular your spending. Luckily, you should be able to reduce your expenditure in the categories below quite easily by following the tips given for each budget category.

Save money on entertainment.

There are several ways you could save money on your monthly or annual amusement and related costs. Here are some of the largest:

- ✓ Please add your dish (satellite) or cable service to Ditch.

- ✓ Saving money on your cell phones or smartphones.

- ✓ Saving money on your internet service.

- ✓ Okay, go to the movies less.

- ✓ Connection Buy fewer books and movies (go to the library instead of:)).

- ✓ Go to fewer and cheaper music concerts.

- ✓ Go to less and less expensive sports games.

- ✓ Investing less in music and computer games.

- ✓ Spend less on mobile gadgets.

- ✓ Cancel subscriptions to magazines and paid TV services (Netflix, Sling, and so on — again, videos from the library are free!).

- ✓ Consider canceling your membership in the gym, community center, museums, aquariums, zoos, and the like.

- ✓ Spend less money on outdoor sports such as hiking, bowling, miniature golf, playing arcades, and so on.

- ✓ Spend less on Christmas shopping.

- ✓ Spend less on family vacations.

✓ Decrease the amount assigned to your personal monthly spending money (your fun money or blow money).

Save money eating out.

The average family in America spends around $3,000 a year eating out. That means there's a lot of money you can save here! I know it might sound crazy, but we spend less than $300 a year eating out. And I don't feel deprived of that! You want to know why? The reason is that frugality has made it possible for us to be able to achieve the other financial objectives that we have — and to do so on one average income.

The best thing you can do to save money by eating out is to do less. But there are a lot of other ways you can save money by eating out, too! Read this article to learn how to save money by eating out.

Save money on groceries.

There are so many of them — so many! — Things you can do to reduce your grocery spending. I 'm talking about more than 70 ways that you can save money on food in this post.

But here are some of the things that you can do to save the most money:

- ✓ Using a meal plan.

- ✓ Link Create a list of grocery stores and follow it.

- ✓ Using a cheat sheet to compare supermarket costs.

- ✓ Shop at discount and rescue grocery stores.

- ✓ Saving money on meat.

- ✓ Saving money on the produce.

- ✓ Spend less money on soda, juice, sweets, snacks, alcohol, and so on.

- ✓ Buy food products when they're on sale and in season.

Save money on transportation.

Another way you really need to be smart with your money is to spend your money on transport. The average car payment in America is nearly $500 a month! Is there any wonder that nearly 80 percent of Americans are living a paycheck? Our savings accounts, emergency funds, and retirement funds are in our garages!

So here's what you can do to turn things around and save money on the cost of transport:

- ✓ Get rid of your car payments and start buying your cars with cash! (This one thing alone could help you become a millionaire! Woo hoo!

- ✓ Become a family of one-cars.

- ✓ Linkless to Drive.

- ✓ Save money on petrol with devices like GasBuddy.

- ✓ Saving money on car maintenance and repairs.

- ✓ Shop around to get the best deal on your auto insurance policy.

- ✓ Drive the speed limit.

- ✓ Wash your own car.

Save money on housing.

Housing is the single biggest burden for many families. But there are also a lot of things you can do to save money on rent. Here are some of my best tips for saving your housing money:

- ✓ Shop around to see if you can lower insurance premiums for homeowners.

- ✓ Look at refinancing your home if interest rates have fallen. (But don't lengthen the term of your loan! If anything, make it shorter!)

- ✓ If you're going to rent, find a cheaper spot.

- ✓ If you bought too much home, look at the downsizing.

- ✓ If you really want to save money on housing, consider renting a spare bedroom (or bedroom) either in the long term or on sites like Airbnb and Booking.com.

- ✓ Saving money on alarm monitoring with low-cost services like SimpliSafe.

Save money on utilities.

You can raise your energy bill very significantly if you want to. I heard from a professor of economics who couldn't afford to see the money that was spent on utilities going down the drain because he knew what the money would grow when it was spent, so he kept his AC up and his stove down, and his family was wearing sweaters and bundled up during the winter and found a way to keep cool during the summer.

We haven't had the drastic in my family (not yet, anyway:)), but it's a little tempting! Because I hate spending money on things that don't have lasting value, too! Sigh. Sigh. In any case, here are some free and simple ways to save money on your utility bill:

- ✓ Turn down (at 62 degrees or lower, if you can) and turn up your AC (at 78 degrees or higher, if you can).

- ✓ Wash all your clothing in cold water. Washing machines are so strong these days that only cold water can keep your clothes clean.

- ✓ Hang your clothes out to dry.

- ✓ Use your dishwasher less. Wait until it's complete and start using your dish drain and washing the dishes by hand.

- ✓ Switch off cameras, TVs, laptops, radios, night lights, and so on when they are not in use.

- ✓ Affirmative Unplug appliances and electronics when they are not in use.

- ✓ Open your curtains during the day to let the sun warm your house during the winter or keep it closed to keep the sun out to prevent it from being too hot during the summer.

Save money on clothing and shoes.

Some people just love buying designer clothes and shoes. And they look so nice! But so is a paid beach house in retirement. So we're buying most of our clothing, for the kids and us, either in supermarkets or in shops. Right now, our kiddos are young, and they don't know the difference (and I hope that even when they're older, they don't care — and I hope they don't.

My sisters and I also change clothes back and forth for our kids, who are the same ages, which is awesome! I love seeing the clothes my kiddos wore on my nieces and nephews; it brings back such fun memories! If you have family or friends with kiddos the same age as yours, see if you can set up a children's clothing co-op!

5. Comparison shop.

Another super smart thing you can do to be good with your money is to compare the store — on almost everything. When I did this, especially with higher costs like fairly large home and auto repairs, the price difference I was quoted was sometimes shocking! Get the most bang for your buck by calling a few (usually five) places or visiting a few shops before buying or spending money on a service like a vehicle, plumbing, or home repair.

We wanted to make some fairly extensive home improvements this year. And one of the things we've just done was to fix our gutters (they needed it!). And as I always do, I've called out to several contractors who came out and made bids. We ended up paying just under $1,000, and I think they did a terrific job. (As far as we can tell, but we're not construction experts!)

But the difference between the highest bid we got and the lowest bid was over $500! So please, please, always compare the shop, and the more expensive the purchase, the more places you need to compare.

Shortly after we moved to our home (which was a mortgage and had not been lived in for more than a year, maybe two), we found that our water was not draining from our showers. And someone in our church gave us the name of a local plumbing company. They came out, and they wanted us to spend $4,000 to dig a big bush and snake our thread, and I don't know what else. But that's $4,000!

So I called around to several other locations, and we ended up paying about $400 for a smaller company to come out and just augur through our line and clear up the roots that had developed into it and put down some anti-root stuff.

Now, the first company isn't a "bad" company, at least not according to Google and my neighbor. We have a rating of 4.5 stars, with over 2,500 ratings. But I'm never going to use them, that's for sure because they tried to sell us up and go for the most expensive option instead of the cheapest (or at least the cheapest option).

And don't even get me started with the auto mechanic shops, and how critical it is that you compare the shop when you get the car repairs done!

6. Put money where it needs to go to be smart with your money and build wealth.

To place your family on a sound financial footing and eventually create wealth, make sure you do the following things.

Build an emergency fund.

As I mentioned briefly above, it is vital for the well-being of your family that you have a significant emergency fund. I would suggest at least three but preferably six months' worth of expenses invested in your emergency fund.

If you haven't already, make your emergency fund your own dedicated savings account. You might also want to open an account with another bank so that the money isn't too easy to reach if you think you would be tempted to use it for other things than actual emergencies.

Get out of nonmortgage debt.

Once you have at least $ 1,000 in a start-up emergency fund, another smart thing to do with your money is to pay off all non-mortgage debt as quickly as possible.

To get out of debt, first figure out how much you owe on your different debts, such as credit cards, student loans, car loans, department store loans, and so on.

Then decide which method you want to use to get out of debt. Depending on your disposition and what motivates you, I recommend using either the Snowball Debt Repayment Method or the Avalanche Debt Repayment Method. Briefly, with the Debt Snowball method, you pay off your smallest debts first to gain momentum and keep up your motivation. With the debt avalanche process, you first pay off debts with the highest interest rates, and eliminating those higher interest rates may be what keeps you most motivated.

Personally, I 'm suggesting the Debt Snowball strategy, as I think it's a great way to build traction because that's the debt repayment system that we used personally.

When you're out of non-mortgage debt and are properly saving for bigger investments and acquisitions (more on that below) so that you can avoid taking on more debt, work to pay off your mortgage early! Getting mortgage debt-free is great because it's one step closer to absolute financial freedom!

Save for larger purchases and expenses.

After you have paid off your non-mortgage debt, start saving for big expenditures and investments so that you can pay for them in cash to stop going back into debt. Debt freedom = financial freedom = harmony and happiness.

To save on these high costs, I recommend that you set up a range of different savings accounts (also known as sinking funds). We personally have more than 20 different savings accounts for our various financial objectives. You certainly don't have to be that detailed, but I would recommend that each family set up these nine savings accounts:

- ✓ Emergency fund

- ✓ Vehicle maintenance and repairs

- ✓ Vehicle purchase

- ✓ Home down payment

- ✓ Home repairs

- ✓ Furnishings and appliances

- ✓ Christmas and gift-giving

- ✓ Vacations

- ✓ Miscellaneous/other short-term savings

By getting these nine savings accounts and working hard to finance them, you will have the cash you need to take care of all the expenditures that arise.

Start investing for retirement.

Once your non-mortgage debt has been paid off, and you save on the necessary costs above, start investing for retirement. I recommend that, once you're out of non-mortgage debt, you start saving 15% of your retirement income as soon as you can, but at least save 10%.

Remember the awesome power of interest payments and start saving as much for pension as you can as soon as you can.

7. Consider doing overtime, getting a second job, starting a side hustle, and finding other ways to earn more money.

I assume that there are more opportunities to make money today than ever before. And you can do all of these things from the home after you get back from work! Some of my favorite ways to make so much money are listed below.

Do overtime.

Working overtime is one of the easiest ways to make extra money. If your boss provides overtime, consider taking advantage of it. Especially if you're in a position where you're trying to pay off your mortgage, save your emergency fund, or save on a big and important purchase, working overtime is a great way to help you reach those goals more quickly.

Ask for a promotion or promotion.

One of the benefits of asking for an increase or promotion is that you receive additional income for (potentially) doing the same amount of work!

If a number of years have passed since you earned a substantial increase, and particularly if you have been an excellent employee at work, make a list of your successes and achievements, and arrange a meeting with your boss to request a promotion or advancement. Focus on the ways you've earned money or saved the money from the company.

When you realize during the meeting that promotion or advancement is not going to happen overnight, ask yourself what concrete steps you may take over the next year or two to make it a reality. Read this book for more detail about how to apply for promotion or promotion.

Do freelance work.

If you work in a profession that lends itself to self-employed jobs, consider taking advantage of the opportunity to earn extra income. I've been writing, editing and proofreading freelance since before I graduated from college with my English degree and editing a minor, and doing freelance work has not only helped me gain experience in other areas besides what I do for my full-time job but has also sometimes (when I wanted to give it time) brought significant additional income.

If you enjoy writing in the same way, look at freelance writing work. Freelance proofreading is another great option if you love to read and have a good eye to detail. If freelance proofreading is a good opportunity for you, then check out this awesome general proofreading course from my friend Caitlyn at Proofread Anywhere!

Look at indeed.com, monster.com, or your preferred work search site for opportunities.

Do consult or coaching.

Similarly, if you have work experience or expertise that lends itself to it, consider using the expertise to do consulting or coaching work. Consulting areas include a human resource (HR) consultant, a public relations (PR) consultant, a marketing consultant, a business management consultant, and an accounting consultant.

Common fields for coaching include financial coaching, work coaching, personal fitness coaching, and coaching.

Search for real.com consulting and coaching opportunities or your preferred job site.

Start a side hustle.

If you'd rather make money without working another regular job, there are a lot of things you can do to make a little extra income with a side hustle. Some ideas include starting your own small business, turning a hobby into a money-maker, being a software engineer, or driving for Uber or Lyft. Learn how to start a side hustle and find out about the other side hustle and bustle that you can explore.

Start a money-making blog.

The opportunity for substantial revenue is one of the reasons why I started this blog. If you love helping people and enjoying blogging, becoming a blogger could be a perfect fit for you. In addition to the high-income opportunities (check out these impressive earnings reports from bloggers who make $10,000 to $100,000 or more a month!), there are many other advantages of being a blogger, such as being able to be your own boss and work on your own time.

Make money with affiliate marketing.

Affiliate marketing is where you suggest a good or service to others, and, in exchange for your sending business, a company pays you a percentage of the sale they made on the basis of your recommendation. Affiliate marketing can be an excellent way to make extra revenue; those who do it well can make thousands of dollars (or more) a month.

For an excellent course on affiliate marketing, check out Making Sense of Affiliate Marketing by Michelle Schroeder, who spends more than $50,000 a month on affiliate marketing. Michelle's course is the first I purchased when I decided to start blogging.

Get a (second) job.

If you're in a position where the money is tight, or you have a lot of debt, or you just want a bigger hammer to crack your financial goals, then look at the possibility of one of you finding a job or a second job.

If a spouse does not work outside the home, for example, consider whether it would be worthwhile for that spouse to start earning an income (maybe with a job that could be done exclusively from home).

Similarly, if one of you works only part-time, you might want to consider going full-time at least temporarily in order to achieve your financial goals more quickly.

Or consider that a partner is willing to get a second job in the evenings or on Saturdays, for example, and to make more money that way.

Earn passive income.

Some options for earning passive income include creating a product that can be sold, writing a book, creating a money-making podcast or vlog, or developing an online course.

8. Automate your finances.

Another smart thing you can do with your money, which will really help you succeed in your finances, is to automate your finances as much as you can. By automating your finances, you're not left so vulnerable to temptation. And you can work effortlessly to achieve your financial goals, and you can do so without having to make a conscious decision to save or invest or pay off debt every time you get paid.

Right after you get paid, move money immediately to pay additional expenses, to your emergency fund and other savings accounts, and to your 401(k) or Roth IRA. Take care of your financial goals easily by funding them instantly! And then live on what's left.

You can simplify your finances and get paid (by direct deposit); prepare for emergencies, big transactions and expenditures, and so on; pay off your loans (as long as you're not in an adversarial relationship with someone you owe money and); pay bills; save in retirement; save for children's college; and more.

9. Stay out of debt to be smart with your money.

The best way to build wealth and one of the best ways to be smart with your money are to get out of debt first and stay out of debt. That's because when you get out of debt — as Dave Ramsey, one of my favorite personal finance gurus, says — you're releasing your biggest wealth-building tool: your income.

By paying off all your debt — including eventually paying off your mortgage — and then staying out of debt, you'll have all your income to use to meet your needs and build up your wealth instead of the banks. And at the end of the day, you will be able to achieve financial freedom.

INCOME GENERATION ONLINE

From online poker to selling your Beanie Babies collection, there's a lot of common, fast-paced, money-making ideas that always pop up. Are they working? Not really, really. Are you going to make money doing it? Maybe, guy. But you'd probably make more money out of your 9-5 job. It's a guaranteed paycheck, at least then. The reality is there are real ways to make money online – millions of people do it every day. From entrepreneurial digital nomads to smart marketers to up-and-coming entrepreneurs, there are plenty of business ideas you can try out at home using your laptop and a decent internet connection. So we're going to break down how to make money online ... the real way.

1. START DROPSHIPPING

Since we're a drop-in blog, we might as well start our list with one of the most famous ways to make money online. According to Google Trends, the popularity of dropshipping is growing rapidly, highlighting its effectiveness as a way to make money online. With success stories about how an entrepreneur made $6,667 in eight weeks or how a store owner made six figures selling just one product, there's plenty of evidence that dropshipping is a real way to make money online.

In case you don't know what dropshipping is: dropshipping is a business model where you sell a product to a consumer, but the manufacturer stocks, bundles, and delivers the product to your customers on your behalf. With Oberlo, you have access to millions of items that can be added to your store. Oberlo also helps you to give the customer information to your suppliers in just a few clicks instead of doing the job yourself.

The easiest way to make money from online drop-shipping? Most marketers have concentrated on a few marketing strategies: running Facebook ads, making influencers advertise the goods, and sending Direct Messages (DMs) to potential social media customers.

2. TRY PRINT ON DEMAND

Printing on demand is also proving to be a popular option. Graphic designers are moving to a business model to market their designs on apparel and other items in order to help monetize their work. They can create a clear and well-established brand for their company with their unique designs.

Print on demand is close to drop-shipping in the sense that you do not need to carry out an inventory or send goods to your own customers. There are, however, two slight differences. First, you can add branded labels to packages. Second, shipping costs are exorbitant, making it impossible to develop a profitable company unless you charge higher rates or sell larger quantities.

The best way to make money from your on-demand print business? Free channels of marketing. Your best bet will be to advertise your goods free of charge on Instagram, Pinterest, or with inexpensive influencers who convert their audiences well. This will help you make money online instead of breaking into pay-as-you-go marketing platforms like Facebook Advertising.

3. MAKE MONEY WITH AFFILIATE MARKETING

Marketing Affiliate is one of the most popular ways to make money online. Over the years, popularity has risen and dropped, but it is still a successful way to make money online. The best part about affiliate marketing is that you can be an affiliate for almost any company, from Shopify to Amazon, to Uber to FabFitFun.

Affiliate marketing helps you to make a living by endorsing certain brands. When you're a smart marketer, you can earn a commission on purchases by selling retail goods, applications, games, and more. Although receiving a commission can seem low, keep in mind that you may be a multi-brand affiliate and include a number of affiliate links in a single blog post.

When you really want to make money online by affiliate marketing, your best bet is to concentrate on content marketing. By building a blog with a number of content pages, you are essentially creating an asset that you can call your own. The best part of concentrating on content marketing is that if an affiliate program closes down, you can move the affiliate connection to a rival without having a negative effect on your side earnings.

4. START A YOUTUBE CHANNEL

The highest-paid YouTuber is 7-year-old Ryan, who is reviewing toys on his YouTube channel, making him $22 million in 2018. The fifth spot is Jeffree Star, which has made 18 million dollars on YouTube and a record that sells over 100 million dollars in goods a year. His YouTube (and Myspace) fame helped him use its influence to make money online beyond his YouTube earnings.

Your YouTube channel should focus on a single niche so that you can build a strong, loyal audience. For example, you can create makeup tutorials, play video games, review items, teach skills, create prank videos, or something else you think there will be an audience for.

The trick to making money on YouTube is to produce videos that people want to either teach or entertain. You can use a clickbait headline to get viewers to watch, or you can use keywords that are tailored for YouTube search. If you have hit the threshold of 1,000 subscribers, you will legally monetize your channel with YouTube advertising.

5. BECOME AN INFLUENCER

Creating your own personal brand will help you make money online. Did you know that in 2018, Kylie Jenner made $1 million for every Instagram post she sponsored, making her the highest-paid influencer? Although reality stars, artists, and athletes may seem to be the biggest influencers, bear in mind that even smaller influencers may make more money today than they did a year ago.

You need to build a massive follow-up to become an influencer. The best sites to do this: YouTube and Instagram. Some of the largest non-famous influencers have often had their first taste of exposure on these platforms. You might want to check out how to get more Instagram followers if you want to build a large Instagram audience.

To make money as an influencer, you can charge for sponsored content, talk gigs, create your own online store and sell items, add affiliate links to your profile, sell your pictures, sell advertisements on your own podcast, get paid as a brand ambassador, create a book, get paid-for events, and more.

6. CREATE AN ONLINE COURSE

Knowledge sharing is one of the easiest ways to make money online. If you are an expert on the subject, you can monetize your knowledge by creating online courses. You can sell your course to Udemy or, if you already have your own audience, to your own website.

To build a popular and successful course, your best bet is to watch other courses on your subject. Look at the ratings, then. What are the aspects that people praise, and what are the things that people hate? How do you make anything better than what has already been created? Focus on creating content that resolves the biggest complaints while emulating the positive aspects that people love about.

The platform you 're selling your course will determine how best to make money. If you're selling your Udemy course, you don't have to do much to promote it. You can almost set it up and forget about it. You might want to promote it to some blogs or to your own website. However, if the course is hosted on your own website, you may want to run ads to promote the course. You should also create an email list so that you can continue to promote future courses to the same audience.

7. PUBLISH AN EBOOK

It's never been easier to publish an ebook with Amazon KDP. All you need to do is write an ebook, format it, create an ebook cover, publish it, and promote it. Back in 2013, I created a few ebooks on Amazon (all but one down), and even though it didn't make me rich, I still make some money out of it.

You can choose to hire a writer for your ebook, a graphic designer, to design a cover, or a freelancer to format an ebook to help you minimize the work you need to do. It's better if you're focused on keywords based on popular Amazon searches. I always used the Keyword Method, which helps you to find the words people use when looking so that you can craft your title around it.

You can market it in a variety of ways and make money online by selling ebooks. You can give away your ebook for a few days free of charge. This makes you rank high in search results for a few days and get some ratings that make you rank higher for paid listings. Plus, I like to create custom graphics on

Pinterest that match the "Pinterest style" instead of just putting an ebook cover as a pin. This helped me get a few clicks from Pinterest to my ebook.

8. START A BLOG

Blogging is one of the oldest methods of making money online. People who love writing tend to start niche-focused blogs. For example, a blog about procrastination, cars, dropships, toys, etc. is often narrow enough to allow you to build a loyal follow-up, but large enough to cover a lot of ground.

You can start a blog on a variety of platforms, from Shopify (remove the checkout feature, so you don't have to pay your subscription while you create it) to WordPress. When you start your blog, concentrate on very specific keywords in a tight focus and continue to expand to other but related categories as you develop and conquer new spaces. This is going to allow you to develop a massive blog over time.

There are a variety of ways to make money blogging. You should add affiliate links to your posts (don't forget the disclaimer). You can monetize AdSense by strategically positioning ads on your website. Sponsored posts can help you to make money from particular brands, which are popular with bloggers. Bloggers can also sell digital or physical products on their website (note: you can add products from Oberlo to your website). You can also use it to build authority so that you can eventually get speaking gigs, TV deals, or large contracts from clients.

9. CONSIDER FREELANCING

The best way to make money online is to take your present work from 9 to 5 and do it online instead. For example, whether you're a writer, an administrative assistant, a graphic designer, a teacher, a developer, etc., you can take the same skills and find online clients that are searching for them.

There is also a never-ending list of websites for each field of freelance jobs. For example, freelance writers may apply for work on individual online job writing boards, but also on general freelance websites such as Fiverr, Freelancer, Upwork, and all others.

You can look for other transferable skills if you find that your work does not have a direct online source of revenue. To make money online as a freelancer, you need to start building a solid portfolio. That could mean doing some free work with some respected mid-tier brands to get started. When you have a solid portfolio, you will begin to reach out to potential large clients and make more money online. Note, freelancing is a number game: the more customized emails and applications you fill out, the more likely you are to get an answer-back.

INCOME GENERATION OFFLINE

It was 2007 when I was 29. I was freshly married and burned out of my chosen profession. Yeah, it burned out before I even turned 30. For the last five years, I've sold mortgages, and I've been unhappy. In my heart, I knew I wasn't able to do this for the rest of my life. Heck, most of the days, I was wondering if I could do it for the next five minutes.

As I sat in my marketing flyers office, I found myself having more fun at work than I had in months. In fact, I realized that the only time I enjoyed working on mortgages was when I was working on marketing. I began to demonstrate my ideas to other Loan Officers in my office, and they asked if I could make materials for them. I started to think that I should make money offline from home.

I had a company before I knew it. Automated Marketing was born in May 2007. I took my love of design and copy and made it into a small company for myself.

When I began, Facebook was at its infancy, and mostly for college students. MySpace was already in charge of the internet airwaves. Digital marketing was, at best, shallow and, at worst, scammy. I invested my time at various mortgages and real estate offices to produce postcards, brochures, and flyers.

INTERNET BOOM

Then, in what seemed like a flash, they were all online. They all needed a new website. It was necessary to create Facebook pages. There was a need to build online marketing strategies. I've been in love with this new medium for my clients.

You see, the Internet was fresh when I was in college. An email was a new form of communication, and people connected to chat rooms. But even in those early days, I saw the potential for business. It was in those years that I knew I was going to build a business on the Internet. This new idea, called digital marketing, seemed to make my dream come true!

GOING NATIONAL

After working with local clients, I realized that if I wanted to expand, I 'd have to go to a national audience. I was itching to write, too, for some reason. I decided to merge my passion for online business and digital marketing with my conventional offline business. I launched my first blog, Marketing Ideas for Agents, in November 2014.

On Marketing Ideas for Agents, I wrote about all the marketing stuff for the real estate industry. I've been learning about conventional marketing concepts like open houses. I've been learning about digital marketing concepts like email marketing and social media.

I saw incredible growth on my blog by the fourth month. I created a network of Realtors on Twitter, and I started to get to know my audience better. I have been noticed by the major players in the industry. My content was being shared on Facebook, Twitter, and LinkedIn. I've been getting a lot of guests invites to share.

Most importantly, I helped Realtors with new marketing ideas. Every day, I received emails to thank me for my writing and my ideas. I was in heaven, man!

But the number one question I've been asking all the time was, "I love your writing, how can you support me? "I've been grappling for an answer to this. You see, I fell in love with writing by this time. I started blogging, and I gave it three months to see if I liked it. I just didn't like it. I fell in love with it!

I didn't want to go back to creating websites, designing flyers, or writing copies for other people.

But that was the exact thing my niche was asking me to do. And instead of going back to do anything, I've put together a squad. If I were hired for a new project, I would recruit contractors to help me do it. I have a copywriter who writes a brilliant copy and performs project management. I have a web developer working on creating WordPress sites for Realtors. I have two different graphic designers who are trying to make us look fine.

I realized that by having a team working on projects that we could grow, I could do what I loved to do. Write it.

FIRST PASSIVE INCOME

Then in 2015, I had a wonderful opportunity to turn into an online course. I received a lot of email subscribers to my blog by posting a guest. Once I did guest posts, I got a profile that led people to my landing page. This strategy has given me thousands of email subscribers in just a few months.

I figured. Realtors were sick of paying a lot of bucks for leads. I figured they were disappointed that they didn't get leads from their own website. And here, I had a way to get leads from my blog that I could translate into real estate.

I produced my Looks to Leads Real Estate Landing Page Course in April 2015. Finally, 15 years later, my vision of an online company came true! I've combined a traditional in-person business service into an online business. In 2015, the class sold over five figures, which was fantastic! It helped other retailers learn how to get details from their website. I've been so overjoyed!

KEY TAKEAWAYS

There are two major takeaways out of my story.

Focus on a niche

The most valuable thing I learned in 2015 is that you need to focus on a niche. If you try to help all service-based businesses, you will fail. There are so many to concentrate on, and the message is going to get watered down. By focusing on Realtors alone, I was able to speak to them in their language.

I was able to show them that I recognized their issues. Most importantly, I was able to show them that I was the person who helped them solve the problems. If I had been too generic in that message, I would have failed.

Combine offline with online

In my business, I have successfully transformed an offline business into an online business. I think we 're too often focusing on "how can I make money online" and ignoring people who are right in front of us. Look around your community for traditional service-based businesses that you can help with. Then reach out to them and give them your services.

Once you've got a grip on what you're doing, move into an online room. Create your website, whether it's blogging, podcasting, or something else. Then turn it into a national or even an international business!

I think we fail to look at the possibilities in our own culture in our crazy rush to make money working from home. Check out the companies in your field. Look for opportunities to help them out.

Can you provide copywriting, web creation, social media, blogging, or graphic design services? There are a lot of companies that want this help, but they don't want to hire someone full-time to do it. Or they want this support, but they don't know how to find someone who's providing these services. Go conventional, make a poster, and visit your local business.

When you have a few customers, build a strategy to take your offline business online, and scale it up. By combining a traditional in-person business with an online business, the opportunities are limitless!

TIPS FOR BEGINNERS INVESTORS

If you're thinking about making an investment, you 're probably not sure how to get started and what you should be investing in. The world of investment can be very challenging for the first time. In reality, for those who encounter it, it can sometimes be confusing. The following ten tips will help you get started in the world of investments.

1. SET INVESTMENT GOALS

It's time to decide what you're going to get out of an investment. Obviously, your ultimate goal is to make money, but the needs of everyone are different. Things to consider include income, capital appreciation, and capital security. Also, consider your age, your personal circumstances, your financial position.

2. INVEST EARLY

The faster you start investing, the better. For one thing, the faster you start, the less capital you'll need each year to achieve your investment goals. Your earnings will increase over time, so don't be afraid to start saving, even if you're a college student-or better yet, in your last year of high school.

3. MAKE INVESTMENTS AUTOMATIC

Set aside a certain amount of money for automatic spending every month. You can set up automatic new investments through various brokerage service firms and automated investment services such as Wealthfront. By doing so, you 're going to stop stalling and spend regularly.

4. LOOK AT YOUR FINANCES

You need to look at how much money you have to spend before you can start investing. Be rational about this. Make sure you have enough money to pay for your normal monthly bills, loan payments, etc. You don't need a lot of money to start investing, but there are risks. You don't want to miss out on paying those significant bills.

5. LEARN ABOUT INVESTING

Once you've got your finances in order, it's time to start learning about investing. Study basic terminology, so you know how to make coherent choices. Learn about stocks, bonds, mutual funds, and deposit certificates (CD's). Don't forget about other details, including diversification, portfolio optimization, and market efficiency.

6. SET UP RETIREMENT ACCOUNTS

There are many tax advantages to having a retirement account. In some cases, the initial investment is tax-deductible, such as IRA's and 401 K's. Others allow you to pay taxes in advance, but not when you withdraw funds during retirement; these include the Roth IRA (Individual Retirement Arrangement). Also, be sure to find out if your employer matches your personal retirement allowance.

7. BE WARY OF COMMISSIONS

Professionals are going to try to talk to you about buying investments that give them high commissions. Without any serious testing, don't do that. Some so-called professionals are well-known to sell their goods but pay their customers nothing.

8. DIVERSIFY YOUR INVESTMENTS

The economy is always fluctuating, and things are still going up and down. To stop losing too much money when stocks fall, make sure you have a diversified portfolio. That way, you 're going to have some stocks that are rising, even when others are falling. Another option is to invest in foreign markets, as they are particularly different from those in the United States.

9. STUDY YOUR PORTFOLIO

It 's important that you always study your portfolio. What's good for your portfolio now, may not be the best for it tomorrow. It's important to know what you've got and where you may need to make improvements in the future. If the economic climate changes, be prepared to make changes to spending as well.

10. Keep Informed

It's a good idea always to study the markets. Learn about the stuff you've invested in, and look for options that keep up with both consumer dynamics and the global economy.

CONCLUSION

Habits of very effective people are not only a must-read because they are classics, but because the only thing that gives us long-term changes is a habit. Habits of highly effective people. In order to explain the value of any habit, I use several stories and examples. Unlike other more complex personal development books, I delve less into the psychology of our brain and draw the actionable aspect of every idea that makes it easy to understand and apply. The Habits of Highly Successful Persons are a very good first reading, particularly when you are new to personal growth. But as it's such a classic, we could risk rejecting every concept as common sense as we heard it before, or we know it already. Yet the real question is not whether or not you know it, and the question is whether or not you apply it. Most specifically, you often use it enough to call it a habit. So the secret of this book is to turn what you learn into an embodied habit. You should relate them to your business goals and to your relationships with your colleagues. You can use them at home, too. You can use them to strengthen your relationship with your parents, your spouse, or your children. Whatever you try to do in life, whoever you want to be, the habits will help you on your journey. You'll be highly effective.

CPSIA information can be obtained
at www.ICGtesting.com
Printed in the USA
LVHW011610131020
668700LV00011B/1305